OF GUTS AND GRACE

FIFTY YEARS WITH
MEN FOR MISSIONS INTERNATIONAL

by

Carroll Ferguson Rader

- The MFM Pledge -

I will do whatever God asks me to do;

I will go wherever God asks me to go;

I will give whatever God asks me to give.

CONTENTS

Prologue

DEDICATION

To the thousands of MFMers whose names do not appear in these pages is this book dedicated, in honor of their sweat, their tears, their unflinching dedication to getting out the Good News.

And to Stella Henry Ferguson as well, whose sweetness, stamina and Christian grace kept husband Dwight (more often than not) aimed in the right direction and focused on what matters most.

OF GUTS AND GRACE:
Fifty Years of Men For Missions International

PROLOGUE

Jim Miles sat motionless on the crude bench; his intense brown eyes missed nothing. On tour in Colombia, South America, with other lay Christians like himself, he awaited the onset of worship. They had told him this ramshackle building was a church, a makeshift village sanctuary where Colombians found God. Jim was a new believer, having accepted Jesus as Lord only a few weeks before.

A small boy wriggled onto the rickety bench beside Jim and fastened his gaze on the foreigner who had invaded his world. "His eyes looked through me, searching for some sign of my love for him," Jim remembers.

"I couldn't restrain my right arm. It reached across his shoulders and drew him closer."

The well-groomed salesman from Indiana immediately caught sight of his new friend's untied, dangling shoestring and reached down to tie it for him.

"But the strain I put on it was too much. It snapped, leaving a piece in my hand," Jim says. "The boy was heartbroken. He shunned my every attempt to tie the string together." Jim felt he'd blown his opportunity to make a new friend and perhaps to share his faith with him. After all, that is why he had come.

As Jim gazed down at his own shoes, sturdy brown oxfords bought for the trip, the solution hit him.

"My new laces came out of my shoes, and I put them into the eyelets of the boy's shoes. Then I put his old knotted strings into my shoes. My feet felt strangely secure. And the boy's spontaneous smile of gratitude gave me a clue about the reason why missionaries were down here in the first place." And the follow-up wonder to the case of the broken shoelace is that during the invitation to accept Jesus as Savior, Jim watched as his little friend's mother walked forward to do just that. To be born again, into the family of God.

Men For Missions International is the conduit, which connected Jim with his small Colombian friend and separated him from his shoelaces. Men For Missions International (MFMI) is the laymen's voice of OMS International, a hundred-year-old interdenominational faith mission once known as The Oriental Missionary Society.

It all began at the dawn of the twentieth century among some telegraphers, Christian laymen, in Chicago who sensed God wanted more from them than their tithe and their weekly presence in church.

To be precise, however, it began with a woman.

Lettie Cowman, a turn-of-the-century lady of refined tastes, came to faith through the influence of an opera singer in Chicago. She told Charles, her husband, of her encounter with God and he too accepted Jesus as his Savior. Charles spoke of his experience to a co-worker at the telegraph office, and soon Ernest Kilbourne joined the family of God.

Under the influence of the shameless, fearless witness of Cowman and Kilbourne, a large segment of the 500 telegraphers with whom they worked found joy, peace and acceptance in Jesus Christ. But the story doesn't end there.

The Cowmans heard A. B. Simpson, founder of the Christian and Missionary Alliance, pour out his heart of concern for those around the world who live in ignorance of God's plan for their salvation. Simpson's urging his listeners to consider taking this good news beyond their borders stirred Lettie and Charles to action.

Responding to Simpson's appeal for funds for missionary work, Charles donated the contents of his pay envelope and his gold watch while Lettie surrendered her wedding ring into the offering plate.

But God wasn't yet finished with the Cowmans. Simpson's final challenge went beyond tangible wealth; he asked for lives, people willing to go wherever God sent them. Charles and Lettie said yes, and the events that followed on the heels of that hundred-year-old yes changed the course of history in uncounted lives on every continent in God's beloved world. Little did the Cowmans know that their covenant with God would produce The Oriental Missionary Society as well as the seed bed from which sprang Men For Missions, the laymen's voice of OMS.

Chapter One

1950s: Where Are the Men?

Dwight Ferguson sighed as he dragged his lanky frame out of the car. A. J. and Jean Herald had insisted that he go with them to hear a missionary speak at their mid-week service. How could he say no to such dear and hospitable friends? How could they know that he had had his fill of missions? That the world and its spiritual needs relentlessly pressed in on him, and all he wanted was to forget about it? This stopover in Ocala, Florida, with the Heralds was turning into a nuisance. He yearned to go home to his Ohio farm and recover from the days of preaching before crowds of people in Cuba, Jamaica, Haiti, Dominican Republic and Puerto Rico.

Wasn't that enough, for goodness' sake?

Nevertheless, the three friends settled into their seats in the little church and turned their attention to what Harold Brabon, OMS missionary to Colombia in South America, had to say. Brabon hammered away at the imbalance between America's opportunities to hear the Christian gospel and those of the rest of the world; just what the weary evangelist did not want to hear yet again. Dwight sneaked looks at his wristwatch trying to figure how early in the morning he could leave without insulting his friends.

At the door, however, Brabon, the missionary, said to Ferguson, the evangelist, "You must call Eugene Erny. He'll want to hear about your time in the Caribbean." Brabon, no mean evangelist himself, knew how to press home his purposes and he told Dwight that Erny was nearby and would want to talk with him.

Befuddled as to why Erny needed to hear about his trip, nevertheless Dwight accepted the information from Harold who, perceiving Ferguson's confusion, reminded him that Eugene Erny was president of The Oriental Missionary Society.

Lord, what are you trying to say to me? Dwight found himself yet again confronted with the world beyond his normal confines...God's waiting world. What was that to a successful, well-known American evangelist? Wasn't responding to calls to preach in the towns, cities and campuses of the United States sufficient?

Ferguson fought to fend off the constant bombardment against his heart and soul by the world beyond his usual borders. But the discomfort of the barrage of information and the emotion generated by the attack were penetrating even his tough hide. And now he was supposed to seek more trouble by phoning the president of a missionary society?

But phone he did and, bewildered by his own contradictory behavior, Dwight Ferguson agreed to meet with Eugene Erny in Rome, Georgia, on his way home to Ohio the next day. In his book, *Motivated Men*, Ferguson later described in his florid prose what took place.

"Our conversation was light, turning often to the Caribbean evangelistic circuit which had just ended. But I was beginning to feel again the hot breath of the Hound of Heaven when Dr. Erny suddenly interjected a new thought. Leaning toward me he paused for a moment then blurted out:

"'Dwight, I think you should expand the blessings of your recent series of laymen's meetings and take a trip around the world.'

"I swallowed hard. The patient, omniscient God was continuing His gentle prodding of me, such an unworthy creature.

"For two hours I listened to the missionary, but I was hearing God's voice. I sensed that my life would never be the same again. Priorities would have to be shifted. Price tags would have to be rewritten. Previous objectives would have to be scrapped to make room for expanded goals demanding abundant resources, greater dimensions of compassion, and a militant but awesome series of challenges. The green light was flashing on and off.

"It was fantastic! I was financially broke with no prospect of a windfall large enough to bankroll Dr. Erny's wild suggestion. Yet reckless faith laughs at impossibilities, and I began envisioning myself traveling around the world with a group of laymen as a Jesus witness."

Buried in Ferguson's telling of the encounter, like yeast in bread dough, lie two phrases that define the story's outcome. "Laymen's meetings" and "a group of laymen as a Jesus witness" prophesy what was to come.

In 1901, the same year that The Oriental Missionary Society came into being, Dwight Harry Ferguson was born in Chicago, eldest of five siblings; a brother and three sisters followed him into the family. The son of a preacher noted for Scripture memorization, Dwight grew into a gangly six-footer with a mind of his own. His sister, Mable, shook her head over his rebellious ways and called him, as a little sister might, "bad." He never conformed to the conscientious, buttoned-up ways of his parents and the people they knew at the Moody Tabernacle where they worshipped.

Dwight preferred to swim at the local indoor pool where future Olympic champion and movie star Johnny Weismuller trained. While hanging out at a neighborhood livery stable, he discovered he liked fast horses; then someone introduced him to motorcycles. Whatever moved fast or called for action attracted the restless young man who could not seem to apply himself to the desk and books at school.

He did like, however, the music and musicians he found at the tabernacle and joined the tenor section in their choir. The strong personalities of musicians and preachers plus the passion they brought to their ministry caught his attention. This did not keep him from abandoning Chicago for North Dakota, though, where he hired on at a cattle ranch. His experiences there flavored his interests and illustrated his preaching ever after, even though his cowboy career ended abruptly. Dwight's concerned father doggedly sought out his elder son and persuaded him to attend a Kentucky camp meeting in a little Bluegrass town called Wilmore and check out a Christian college there, which was named for famed English evangelist Francis Asbury.

The implacable courage of his father and the spiritual power that confronted him at Asbury College changed the course of Dwight Ferguson's life. "This is the place for me," he decided. Despite his lack of a high school diploma he enrolled in the school. "Oh, yes," he used to say. "I studied in the academy (Asbury's high school), in the college, and in the seminary." Studied, yes; gained any diplomas? No.

One asset he did gain, however, did more for him than the finest education available. Straight-backed Stella Henry, a spirited Ohio farm girl and former teacher in a one-room schoolhouse, enchanted Dwight from his first glimpse of her. He knew he had to have her and set out with all the charm and determination he could muster to win her. Stella shrewdly examined the city boy from Chicago and listened to his talk, both as he preached as one of President Henry Clay Morrison's student evangelists and as he murmured in her ear his love and regard. She decided she loved him, too. Thus God put together a remarkable partnership that blessed and influenced people across North America and around the world for more than fifty years.

In the months that followed Ferguson's encounter with Eugene Erny, he fulfilled preaching engagements already promised while at the same time breathing life into the sparks struck by their conversation. Preach in the Orient? In India? Opportunities to point spiritually hungry people to Jesus made his blood run hot like no other adventure he tried. This stood true ever since his Asbury days when Dr. Morrison sent him out with a tent and orders to preach Christ. It gathered momentum as he rode horseback through Mexican underbrush as a summer missionary before anyone knew what that term meant. While he pastored in Tacoma, Washington, the corridors of the local jail drew him to the men and women behind its doors and bars more powerfully than did his Sunday pulpit. He copied his Salvation Army acquaintances by preaching in street meetings. So why not take the good news that fired his soul to the rest of the world? Why not move through the doors that swung wide before him? And, ever the tablehopping, gregarious people-person that he was, Dwight wondered why not take another guy with him?

One of Ferguson's preaching commitments was in Lima, Ohio, an event that God had in mind from the outset. In Lima lived Stanley Tam, who was about to find the course of his life changed forever. Tam tells about it in the book, *God Owns My Business*, where he describes Ferguson's invasion of Lima "for a two-week crusade sponsored by our church. Though participating on the steering committee, I had never heard of the man and, being quite busy, complained a bit to my wife about our evenings being tied up for so long a time.

"But this was no ordinary man.

"For the opening nights he spoke only to Christians. He did not follow the usual procedure of haranguing church members to shreds, but with power and compassion he expounded from the Scriptures the place of the Holy Spirit in the life of a believer.

"On the fifth night I went to the altar. Pride had crept into my life, complacency, self-satisfaction. I asked God to empty me of self, of pride, and to let the Holy Spirit fully control my mind and body.

"It was a time of dynamic renewal in my Christian experience.

"The speaker and I became close friends, and as the conclusion of the meetings drew near, he startled me by saying he planned a trip to Formosa, Korea, and Japan, and wanted me to go along to give my testimony as a Christian business-man."

Tam admits he "didn't take the idea seriously." Undaunted, though, Ferguson wrote him every week—nagging, urging, cajoling. Tam and wife Juanita debated often whether this was a man's whim or God's plan. Juanita finally told Stanley to look at it as a businesslike check into what was happening with funds they'd invested in missions.

"Okay, let's put it this way," Stanley conceded. "I'll plan to go unless something happens to make the trip impossible."

Inevitably, several things did happen. Family deaths and the loss of an indispensable secretary caused Tam to tell Ferguson he could not go. Ferguson wrote back, "It is vitally important for you to go. God has given you the gift of being able to express yourself to other laymen who can stimulate others in the task of world evangelization." Ferguson had come to this conclusion via his own pilgrimage. He too had battled distaste for what he knew the Lord had in mind and struggled against God's pressure on him to obey. Having surrendered at last to divine leadership, Dwight did not give up in the face of Tam's refusals. He knew better than most what was at stake and remained unapologetically dogmatic in his insistence as to what Stanley Tam should do.

According to missionary author Ben Pearson, Tam refused Ferguson's invitation one time too many. Dwight was preaching in Temperance, Michigan, and Tam drove over from Lima to tell the evangelist he could not go. The harried businessman said, "Dwight, stop your planning! I'm not going with you!"

Courtesy required he attend the service, however, and between the powerful nudges of the Holy Spirit and Ferguson's blunt response to Tam's refusal, the man didn't stand a chance. Dwight had said to him, "All right, Stan, if you don't want the blessing, God will give it to somebody else."

"That settled it," Pearson wrote. "Stanley did not want to miss the blessing! He decided to go for six weeks only...to give a brief, straight-from-the-shoulder businessman's testimony in each service."

That fall Stanley boarded a plane with Dwight along with musicians Aileen and Byron Crouse, and headed across the Pacific Ocean toward Taiwan.

"I'll never forget the flight," Tam says. "Dr. Ferguson is a most amiable man, warmly human, engagingly genuine. He has the gift of motivating and molding people by helping them recognize their latent potentials. He encouraged me to look for widening opportunities to stimulate laymen in the full stewardship of their lives."

Pearson, in *Men Plus God,* amplifies Tam's description of the evangelist: "Dwight, as everyone calls him, a man with a tangy tongue, a salty vocabulary, a penetrating wit, and a slightly nasal, almost New England twang had gotten the evangelistic party together for his first around-the-world campaign."

In Taiwan just a few days later, however, tragedy fell in on the team like a rockslide on a tent. The evangelistic party,

Tam and the Byron Crouses encircled Dwight Ferguson, their leader, as he sat stunned by news from Stella via an overseas phone call. His precious 21-year-old son Marvin lay dead. Killed in a hunting accident in Colorado. Dwight Ferguson, just embarked on the mission of persuading men to take Christ to the world, had lost the young man dearer to him than any other.

Ferguson left Tam and the Crouses to fulfill the Asian schedule while he boarded a plane back to Ohio to bury his only son. He later admitted to wrestling with God and his own breaking heart as the plane droned across the Pacific. Meanwhile, Tam and the Crouses soldiered on without him, assuming responsibility for the schedule of meetings in Taiwan, Korea and Japan. Tam, the layman, now had every prop provided by the experienced evangelist knocked away. Through an interpreter, fumbling along, he tried to share his faith in Jesus Christ so his hearers might accept the Savior, and live.

As the decades marched on from that watershed September in 1952, opportunities for lay Christians to work hand in glove with God poured in beyond anything Dwight Ferguson and his friends imagined possible. Countless men and, yes, women opened their hearts in obedience to God.

The final Ferguson-Tam debate about the Orient trip took place in Temperance, Michigan, where Dwight preached an area-wide evangelism campaign for the local Youth For Christ committee and a businessmen's group. While there, he stayed in the home of Eleanor and Harry Burr, a pair of career-oriented Christians who stayed busy in their community seeking to point their neighbors to Christ. They gave leadership to the campaign, which turned into a genuine revival marked by repentance, redemption and Holy Spirit-generated power.

As was the case with the Tams following Ferguson's meetings in Lima, friendship flourished between the evangelist and the Burrs, a pattern that marked Dwight's life throughout his years of revival ministry across mid-America. He often dropped by their home for more of the special brand of hospitality they offered, and to share over ice cream, perhaps, what the Lord was currently pressing in on his spirit.

Harry Burr remembers, "Stella and Dwight went to India in 1952 (this occurred a few months after Marvin's death) and while there Dwight discovered something that really bothered him. On the plane home he thought about the fact that in India women missionaries outnumbered the men working there, seven to one. 'Where are the men?' he moaned."

Ferguson did not think women would fail to get the job done, nor did he believe they were not authorized to try. Not at all. He liked women, believed in them, appreciated and admired them for all their gifts and graces, whether called to public Christian ministry or as less visible tools in the hands of the Creator. His love and respect for his Stella shone out strong and obvious; he depended on her for more than he could articulate and she never let him down.

But old-fashioned attitudes shaped Dwight's thinking about women. He believed in gallantry and chivalry, that men should step up and take responsibility for the bigger jobs. Behind the outward symbols of hat-removal and door-opening stood his commitment to digging the ditches, driving the trucks, and lifting the weighty end of the load. Yet never did he turn his back just because some woman proved strong enough to do these things in the absence of a man. He told Harry how he wrestled in prayer over the problem.

"Where are the men?" he asked the Lord repeatedly. This question drove him for years to come and "MFM was born," according to Harry, "as God pushed him to do something about it."

Male absence when the big jobs loomed bothered him. It had nothing to do with the rights or wrongs of women preaching or teaching, with their assuming leadership; it was about wiring and shoveling and hammering. About taking hold of that heavy end rather than sitting at ease on the couch back home and letting the "little woman" assume sole responsibility for Christ's last command to His church--to teach all nations about redemption and peace.

Harry Burr, Christian layman and Dwight's friend, knew the turn the evangelist was taking in his preaching. "The messages from Dwight's lips in camp meetings and special services started going out," he remembers. "'You need to ask God what he would have you do instead of just being selfish.'"

Ferguson personalized his message for Harry. "His words to me? He underlined Psalm 2:8. 'Ask of me and I will make the nations your inheritance, the ends of the earth your possession' (NIV). Then he put a little note there beside it. 'Why don't you?' He was telling me to start asking God for the nations. I didn't know what to do. I prayed much about it."

Each summer OMS held a missionary conference at Winona Lake's Bible Conference facility in Indiana. Following Dwight's capitulation to the Lord's direction to include the world in his ministry, he and Stella began to aggressively urge their friends to attend with them. Convinced that everyone else would experience the joy and spiritual stimulation they found in the fellowship of others with like worldviews, they cajoled people like the Burrs into giving it a try.

"Eleanor and I went," Harry says, "and became acquainted with OMS. We found a group small in numbers but could not believe the wonderful spirit among mostly old ladies and men who came. We were among the young ones, only in our late twenties, but we were excited about the potential."

In July 1953, Dwight Ferguson, burning with his God-lit vision to involve men in worldwide evangelism, asked for a spot on the convention program where he and a couple of laymen could unburden themselves. Receiving permission for an afternoon session, Dwight Ferguson, Stanley Tam and undertaker Ronald DuFresne, a Ferguson friend from the Northwest, in pungent, unadorned prose articulated the world vision burning in their souls. It was the first time laymen—not professional missionaries, not ordained clergy people—ever spoke at an OMS convention.

God honored the session, laying groundwork for a movement that forever altered the mission profile and way of doing His business. Interestingly enough, when the offering buckets went 'round, people put into them the largest offering ever seen to that point in an OMS meeting. Greece missionary Paul Pappas, so moved by what he heard, donated his Kentucky home to the cause.

In 1954, at the Winona Lake OMS convention, Ferguson, still charged with the conviction that men must involve themselves in missions, could contain himself no longer. As

Harry Burr says, "God put his hand on Dwight Ferguson, who stood up in a meeting of a bunch of prayer circle ladies in the Eskimo Inn. He said, 'It's time we start a laymen's missionary movement in the OMS.'

"He told them that if anybody was interested they would meet across the street by a tree and organize a group of men interested in missions."

Shock squelched the routine rustle of breakfast conversation and prayer requests. In the silence, chairs began to scrape back from tables. Intrigued men, one by one, followed Dwight Ferguson out the restaurant door, into the sunshine, across the street to the tree, to participate in the birth of Men For Missions.

OMS President Eugene Erny joined the men under the tree. After all, he had invested time and talk in Dwight Ferguson and the expansion of his evangelistic ministry to a worldwide scope and knew he should remain in touch with his investment.

Ferguson and the men he sought to ignite with love for the Lord's waiting world moved way out on their designated limb without a clue as to what would happen to them there. All they knew was that it was where they belonged and from there they would do what they must...in the Savior's name.

Dwight H. Ferguson
Founder of MFMI
First Executive Secretary
1954-1955

Dale McClain
Executive Director
1955-1956

Chapter Two

1950s: "Of the Holy Spirit"

Eldon Turnidge nodded his dark, brush-cut head when the guys suggested he serve as secretary. His job? To record decisions of the newborn laymen's mission organization now surging toward life in northern Indiana. Later that day Ferguson had led his brigade of men—"Probably 19 or 20 of us, as I recall," says Turnidge—from the shelter of the tree into a meeting room of the Winona Hotel. There, captivated by the idea of a mission channel for men, men who wanted to contribute to spreading God's good news around the world, Turnidge stood ready to grab a corner of the project and do what he could to make it happen.

As recording secretary, Eldon remembers that all he did "was write down the names of the two officers who had been elected." (Which were Lloyd Gallimore, president, and Dwight Ferguson, executive secretary.) "I think I made a list

of the people who were there but I'm not sure of that...."
About Gallimore's involvement in the MFM startup, his
daughter, Martha Easter, remembers, "Dad was very strong
as a Christian layman, and was glad for an opportunity to *do*
something besides just give money."

Turnidge also remembers that Stanley Tam was there,
along with Cleveland banker Roland McGilvray, whose
Asbury College sophomore daughter, Barbara, was in Colombia giving her summer to help the OMS team there.
Several missionaries showed up, too, Eldon recalls, among
them Lee Jeffries, Meredith Helsby, Eugene Erny and others.

Ferguson took charge of the meeting and sought to
convey to that circle of men his burning hunger to see Christian men open themselves to whatever God had in mind for
their participation in worldwide evangelism. "He was the
promoter," Eldon says, "and he did a great job."

If Stanley Tam turned out to be the guinea pig for
laymen learning how to involve themselves in missions, Eldon
Turnidge was the pilot model of a layman contributing his
expertise in the workings of a mission agency, up to and
including top-level administration. He had just accepted an
invitation to serve on OMS's Home Board, the first layperson
to be so trusted.

"A peppermint farmer" is what Dwight called the tanned, smiling Oregonian forever afterward, and in a somewhat simplistic sense he was right. Eldon farmed 600 acres in the Willamette River valley and planted much of that acreage with mint, a lucrative cash crop in the region. Peppermint, however, did not cover the logging business and other enterprises which filled his days.

A stalwart Christian with a good head for business and a strong heart toward God, Eldon and his wife, Mary, went to South America in 1953 to learn more about the overseas mission efforts to which they contributed through their small country church. In Colombia they sought for and then stumbled onto the OMS work in Medellin as they followed up their brief acquaintance with missionary Carol Harding, who had visited their church.

That acquaintance and the others they made in South America, plus Eldon's appointment to the board, promoted for them the idea of attending OMS conference at Winona Lake. All of which, under God's hand, put the Oregon farmer center stage for MFM's debut.

Did the organizing meeting that July afternoon launch the MFM concept onto the evangelical scene as an instant success? Turnidge says, "We all returned home burning with zeal but the ensuing year, except for occasional contacts by Dwight, was fallow and barren."

Harry Burr tells a similar story. He recalls that the men returned to their homes and businesses, Dwight to his preaching schedule. "Not a whole lot was accomplished that first year," Harry says, "but it (MFM) was founded; it was there. Action took place but not in an organized way." Harry also remembers another watershed moment under that tree in Indiana. OMS President Eugene Erny prayed that "this not be an organization but a movement of the Holy Spirit." Time would tell how God honored his prayer.

That original circle of men swelled in number as Dwight Ferguson—passionately, incessantly—did what he did best. He phoned and visited, preached and talked with men about what plain ordinary guys could do to get out the good news around the world. God's pitchman he was and, like any good salesman, he pushed for a decision from his target man. Make a choice. Go and see. Give God a chance to revolution- ize your life. Get a passport. Go to OMS convention. And if the guy wasn't sure he wanted his life revolutionized—rather liking things the way they were—Dwight ignored that wish the same way he brushed aside Stanley Tam's protests and caveats, or Harry Burr's career issues.

Another man who encountered Ferguson's genial buzz-saw approach lived in Mt. Carmel, Illinois. Enloe Wallar was known around town not only for his expertise in oil leases and banks, but also for his wit, wisdom and porkpie hats.

Ferguson and Wallar became acquainted when Dwight preached a series of meetings in the Methodist Church, which turned into a four-alarm, Spirit-fed-and-led, six-week revival in 1950. Wallars and Fergusons forged a friendship in those days that lasted for the rest of their lives.

So what else could Dwight do but pump white-hot enthusiasm from his heart into Enloe's. However, as was often the case, it took a while for Dwight's target man to move his temperature into the red zone, and Enloe was no exception.

He dearly loved the preacher with the piercing blue eyes and pointing index finger that could stab its blunt way right into the crux of the spiritual matter even though its tip veered noticeably to the left. After all, Ferguson's probing sermons on personal encounters with the Holy Spirit had reorganized Wallar priorities entirely.

But missions? Go overseas and talk about your faith? Fly across the ocean in an airplane? Not me, buddy.

Enloe feared flying. Had dreadful nightmares about it. But in 1957, rather than take the easy way and dabble with an organized, accompanied tour to a mission field, he did a remarkable about-face. Seizing his fear in both hands, he arranged to travel around the world on his own, visiting missionaries and learning what they do. Talk about deep end.

Enloe's friend, oilman Jack Houchins, heard about the journey and decided to go along. Thus committed to behavior way beyond their normal southern Illinois comfort zone, the two men set off on a round-the-world odyssey--visiting missionaries, seeing their work, and asking questions. Standing in awe, they shed manly tears at what God was doing in places that until then they didn't know existed.

In honor of Marvin Ferguson's premature death, Enloe and Jack left funds in Taejon, Korea, to build a church in his memory. The building would be dedicated in 1958, shortly after Marvin's sister, Carroll Ferguson Hunt, and husband Everett arrived there to begin their missionary careers with OMS International.

The Wallar/Houchins adventure lasted 80 days; both men returned to the United States far different from when they left. Enloe had surmounted what was probably his last bout of fear. At the trip's beginning in Los Angeles he suffered a panic attack when the enemy of all who obey God whispered, "You'll die, Enloe, in a watery grave."

But Wallar did not fall for that one. Hadn't his friend flown him to Chicago for the shots he needed for their trip? His daughters, Marylin and Fran, remember that he even *liked the ride* in the diminutive private plane.

When all was said and done, 80 days later Enloe Wallar returned as a transformed Christian, ready and willing to do whatever God asked him to do, go wherever God asked him to go, give whatever He asked him to give. Enloe spoke in public about his experiences whenever asked to do so. He and Irene formed a mission prayer group that met in their home. If Dwight Ferguson ever preached in the area, they were there, adding their prayers, gifts and testimonies in support of their friend and the cause of missions that burned in their hearts.

But yes, the first year in the life of Men For Missions was less than remarkable. Much less. Dwight Ferguson preached his way across the country, of course, but in fulfillment of prior commitments to revivals and deeper life sessions.

Nevertheless, he bore down relentlessly on the need for worldwide concern by Americans so blessed materially and spiritually. As he spoke he always found a way to mesh the presence of the Holy Spirit with the fired-up desire to *do* something for those who do without. Or not leaving it to the women's missionary societies or the overworked professionals pouring out their lives far from home.

But all this preaching guaranteed that Ferguson did little as executive secretary to expedite the planning, executing and organizing which MFM needed to stay alive. This was not one of Dwight's strengths. Eldon Turnidge knew they needed a full-time helmsman. "Dwight saw the potential but he didn't see the mechanism to bring it to pass," he says.

In 1955, Ferguson resigned from his executive secretary post because he could not do it justice, and OMS missionary Dale McClain took his place. Small and fiery, McClain, having served in China and India, communicated his passion for missions with vigor and eloquence, but wife Polly's life-threatening ill health held them in the U.S.

In *Men Plus God,* Ben Pearson quotes McClain's definition of the moment: "It was suggested that I assist the men by taking care of some of the details—that's the way I got involved."

Seizing the MFM helm—and its details—when asked, Dale swung into action as if the job had been created just for him. "Things began to move," Harry Burr observes. In the main, "things" included Dale and Dwight speaking in meeting rooms, living rooms, Sunday school rooms and sanctuaries—urging lay people to learn firsthand what mission is all about and to discover their part in it.

Turnidge describes that second coming together of the MFM nucleus. "The next annual convention of OMS found Tam witnessing and Ferguson agitating. Fervor was high and the vision still alive, thank God....The laymen got together again and because of Gallimore's resignation, a call came for the election of a new president. Yours truly had the distinct honor and unusual privilege of being chosen to head MFM. It was my joy," he reflects, "to be a part of MFM—the toddler, MFM—the teenager, and MFM—the adult. I was mightily challenged by the responsibility and the opportunity."

OMS President Eugene Erny wrote to Eldon about his election: "We are so happy that you were elected president of the MFM movement, and we believe under God and your leadership the Lord is going to enable us to go forward in this department."

Just as the MFM head of steam began to build, Polly McClain regained her health and OMS assigned her and Dale to Hong Kong. Now what?

But the McClain appointment did not take God by surprise. Harry Burr's brother, Lawrence, a gifted pastor and college development officer long known as Larry, was aware of the newborn laymen's organization and had watched it carefully since its inception. He had heard Dwight Ferguson preach in Michigan and knew Eldon Turnidge, the Tams, and Dale McClain. He also shared his brother Harry's sense that what was happening was a movement of the Holy Spirit and found himself wanting to join in. He loved lay people and, as Harry says, "believed in their potential to change the world."

McClain saw Larry's skills and talents and said to him, "Larry, would you consider coming to OMS and taking over our laymen's program?"

"I'll sure pray about it," Larry replied. He prayed, and then agreed to tackle the job.

The OMS board in turn approved Larry Burr as leader of Men For Missions. An MFM budget did not exist at that time, so Eldon and Mary Turnidge underwrote Larry's first year, sensitive to, Eldon writes, "the obvious need, and grateful for God's provision."

One of the first things Larry Burr did was call together several of the leader laymen—Eldon Turnidge, president; Bob Martin, secretary; plus Roland McGilvray, Dale McClain, Bill Gillam, and Clyde Taylor in a cabinet session. Their goal? To create guidelines for MFM. Bylaws. Organizational structure. But the Holy Spirit, who seldom uses predictable methods, brushed aside some of what we consider necessary and set in motion His unique methods of achieving such prosaic goals.

Larry describes them almost 50 years later.

"We gathered in the living room on our knees. Prayer was natural and a must. We worked informally on the floor, writing, discussing, planning, and praying back and forth.

"Things began to take shape. We were very aware of the presence of the Holy Spirit. He was in charge, providing us the outline of a revolutionary plan that would awaken men to their obligation to 'go ye,' an opportunity to march back to their home churches ready and willing to be changed.

"They had backed their wives with a few dollars for the Women's Missionary Society, but had left the praying and going largely to them."

Burr knew they knelt on holy ground. "Looking back (I) have flashbacks of goose bumps, excitement, prayerfulness, and drive because our discussions and planning were from the same pages. When we decided this was the day to hammer out directions for the new movement called Men For Missions, God consumed us all. Food was secondary, other concerns were set aside. No one felt competent other than praying for divine intervention to our thought process. Our prayers were audible, co-mingled almost like one voice at times.

"Ideas, fresh thoughts began to flow...notes made and remade, and from our depths came God's plan. No one deserved to say, 'See what we have done.' No one believed we did anything but listen to God.

"Men For Missions was born of the Holy Spirit and could be transmitted one man at a time by the Holy Spirit, using each man who embraced it.

"As we proceeded to final consensus there was a relief. Pressure was off. As we separated we faced a fatigue that was both physical and spiritual. It was grand!"

Larry Burr
Executive Secretary
1956-1960

Harry G. Burr, Jr.
International Executive Director
1960-1983

Chapter Three

1950s: Men For Missions Stays

Larry Burr began pouring forth ideas as to how men could share responsibility for getting God's good news to the ends of the earth. Meanwhile, Harry and Eleanor Burr's budding commitments to obey God tore through their comfortable lives like a tornado through Kansas.

This was inevitable, it seems. After all, back when Dwight Ferguson was dropping by their Michigan home on his way to and fro and leaving the Bible open to the psalm where it says, 'Ask of me and I will give you the heathen for your inheritance,' he turned up the heat by penciling in, "Why don't you?"

About as subtle as a bulldozer, but in this case, most effective. Thanks to Dwight's nagging, the Burrs attended the OMS convention and what they heard that first summer prompted them to volunteer for missionary service. Their lack of formal Bible training sank that idea with mission hierarchy, so they went home to growing business success and heavy involvement in their church and denomination. All good, all profitable...but the dissatisfaction, the urge remained. Harry then quit the insurance business, walking away from three agents who answered to him and a boss who dangled before him a higher salary as incentive to stay.

Harry tells what happened next in *Iron Sharpens Iron*. "The next night Eleanor and I went to a Men For Missions banquet in Dayton, Ohio. As we walked into the hotel, Enloe Wallar, a charter MFMer, met us at the door. 'Harry, it's great to see you. Could I ask you a question?'

"'Sure, Enloe, why not?'

"'Have you ever considered quitting your job with the insurance company and coming with OMS?'

"Of course Enloe didn't know I had just resigned...I guess I was toying with him a bit when I said, 'Well, I'll pray about it.'

"The next afternoon I was asked to accompany 15 men to the clothing store of Nate Scharff there in Dayton, for prayer. We went to a second-floor room and although we prayed for almost two hours, it seemed like 20 minutes. We were the recipients of a wonderful outpouring of the Holy Spirit, and during that time God sealed a decision in my heart. We would join OMS."

While awaiting approval of their application by the OMS board they put their house up for sale and drove to Winona Lake, Indiana, to volunteer their services. This meant commuting between Findlay, Ohio, and Winona Lake for the weeks they waited. In June 1957, news of their acceptance came down from the mission board...and hard on the heels of this word, their roof caved in.

Eleanor, in the throes of leaving her dream house, had to be hospitalized for an infection where treatment by penicillin nearly killed her.

A missionary borrowed Harry's new Plymouth and wrecked it.

Another missionary—also borrowing—threw a rod through the engine of Eleanor's car.

At the hospital "I asked Eleanor how she felt," Harry writes in *Iron Sharpens Iron*. "Tears rolled from the sides of her tightly swollen eyes as she said, 'I've never felt more at peace. I believe we're in the center of God's will.'"

Shortly after the Burrs' personal storm abated, OMS asked Harry to take Dale McClain's job as regional director for the eastern United States, because Dale and Polly were needed to direct mission efforts in Hong Kong. In 1957, Larry Burr, infusing MFM with life and growth, and Harry Burr, learning the regional ropes from Dale McClain, worked out of the same regional office in Winona Lake for some months before Men For Missions moved to OMS headquarters in Los Angeles.

Energetic innovation marked the years of Larry's leadership of Men For Missions. Slim and dark-eyed, with a ready grin, he injected all he did with high intensity, deep spirituality, and obvious joy. "Every day was exciting," Larry says in retrospect. "God permitted me to catch dreams and visions that could help advance the cause."

The list of ways for men to participate in getting the gospel out to the world grew almost daily, it seemed, and included:

- cars provided by Christian dealers for OMS missionaries, both overseas personnel on furlough and homeland staffers
- councils in communities across the U.S. and into Canada where men gathered in fellowship to learn about and pray for missionaries and their work
- yearly building projects funded and constructed by MFMers, beginning in Ecuador
- coin and stamp collecting to earn project money
- by 1956, *Action* magazine, MFM's own periodical
- laymen's day at OMS convention, beginning in 1957

Eldon Turnidge inspired what was to become a core ingredient of the MFM mystique when he persuaded five men to join him in 1957 on what he called an "exposure in Ecuador and Colombia."

One of the five was Archie Porter of St. Petersburg, Florida, who Eldon met at OMS conference and invited to join the tour. But Archie's part of the MFM story began—not surprisingly—some months earlier in an encounter with Dwight Ferguson. Archie heard about Ferguson from George Passmore, one of the salesmen in his Venetian blind company.

"Archie, I know a man you just gotta hear preach on the Holy Spirit," George told him.

Archie agreed to go with George the next night to Northside Methodist Church in St. Pete where Dwight, just returned from India, poured out his passion for those who haven't heard the name of Jesus.

"We went to the altar," Archie and wife Mary Lou remember, "asking how to make up for lost time."

Ferguson stood at the Porter front door the next morning. He had seen spiritual hunger and strength in Archie and Mary Lou, and he coveted them for the cause of missions. Dwight launched into his sales pitch, trying to convince them to attend OMS convention up in Indiana. They succumbed to his fervor—as did so many others—and made the trip. When Turnidge met Archie there, he talked about the "trial balloon" trip he was planning to South America "to see what laymen could do."

"I'll pray about it." Archie used every Christian's most reliable way around making a difficult decision. Back in St. Petersburg, however, he made a tactical error when he phoned Dwight, who then lived in the same city, to tell him about Eldon's idea.

Ferguson again stood at Archie's door, crackling with excitement. "Do you have a passport?" he questioned.

"No."

"You should get one...just in case."

Mystified by his own behavior, Archie acquiesced and got his passport.

"Who is your doctor, Arch?"

"Why?"

"It'd be nice to have your shots...in case."

Archie obediently got the shots necessary for travel in South America and then told Eldon he would join the trip.

"I've never been the same," Archie acknowledges, and neither has MFM. Since 1957, thousands of people—men and women—have acquired passports and shots and trekked off in all directions to see firsthand what missions are all about. And they never go to just stand and stare in curiosity at what they've never seen before. Instead, they discover what a missionary really does all day. Then they break out their own work clothes and lay brick, hammer nails, build roads. At the end of long, hot days they go to God's outposts to worship with Latino, Asian, islander or European believers. And they often stand with wobbly knees to tell, line by line with a translator's help, how Jesus changed their lives and made them new.

While moving through such adventures they always glean names and needs to add to their prayer lists—or even create one where there was none—for they discover that upon boarding the plane for home, they left part of themselves behind.

Decades later, 15 trips later, Archie tries to explain: "I was wrapped up in my city, but I discovered the world...everything changed."

Change became commonplace for the Porters from the moment they knelt together following Dwight's impassioned plea that they consider the world and its needs. They began inviting friends and neighbors to their home for monthly meetings that back missionaries with prayer and thousands of dollars each year. They also launched into a hospitality lifestyle, making hundreds of missionaries welcome as they traveled through Florida.

They made their first faith promise in consultation with Dwight and Stella who had become cherished friends, the four of them bonded in their mutual concern for world evangelization. Archie committed a tithe of the profits from his small Venetian blind business and designated that, to begin with, to the support of Fergusons' daughter and son-in-law, Carroll and Everett Hunt. Hunts were headed to Korea as OMS missionaries.

But that isn't all. Archie, a man of prayer, asked the Lord a pivotal question: "Some men can do useful stuff, Lord. What can *I* do?"

"What do you have in your hand?" came back His question.

"Venetian blinds."

Archie phoned OMS headquarters to offer window coverings...for the world. Literally. For the next 35 years the Porters provided top quality shades and blinds for homes and offices, schools and clinics in countries where OMS works, as well as in the homeland.

"Our company was small," Archie claims. "I had only one employee when I started."

He sold the business some 41 years later, complete with a much larger plant and 97 workers. But the best part is that the new owners continue supplying window coverings whenever Archie asks them to.

Another Floridian heard Dwight Ferguson preach in the 50s. Porters, saturated by the Holy Spirit with a passion for people without their Savior, took Flo Rickards to Lake of the Palms for an MFM retreat. Before the car wheels stopped turning, Larry Burr walked up to greet Archie and Mary Lou. Then he poked his head through the back window and said to Flo, "I understand you're my new secretary."

"Who are you?" Flo blurted. They'd never met.

It didn't stop there. Flo had agreed to sing a mission-themed duet with Mary Lou for one of the sessions. "Lord, Send Me There." Overwhelmed with the incessant emphasis on mission to which she'd so recently been subjected, Flo broke down on the second stanza, and then bolted from the meeting. Mary Lou persevered through the song while Flo sobbed in her room.

The outcome? Flo "settled it with God," quit her travel agency job and took up her post in March 1959, as secretary to the director of Men For Missions in their new offices at OMS headquarters in Los Angeles. When asked why, Flo quotes the verse, "I'd rather be a doorkeeper in the house of my God than dwell in the tents of the wicked" (Ps. 84.10 NIV). Which isn't to say that Flo's travel agency was a tent of the wicked; it does affirm that the Lord gave her a servant's heart and a pair of willing, oft-utilized hands for her more than 18 years of service.

Did she regret the change? Apparently not. "They made me feel appreciated," she asserts. "Like a queen. We worked side by side.

"The Lord always rewarded me," she says of her countless hours of overtime. No resentment there. "We had a ball!"

With Flo in place to keep applying grease to the wheels, Larry Burr moved into a second year directing Men For Missions in high gear. "More" seemed to be the operative word to describe those times. More men with the world on their hearts. More councils, more prayer meetings, more banquets. Larry went wherever invited and when he preached, audiences often heard a recurring theme that spelled out the purpose of MFM simply, clearly. It became identified as its heart, its core, forever after. Larry charged his hearers to dare to go anywhere God told them to go—do anything God told them to do—give anything God told them to give.

This three-pronged creed rolls off the tongue as easily as a nursery rhyme, but the living of it could challenge a spiritual Olympian. Now, to do—go—give, as God orders, is the only requirement for membership in Men For Missions. The word passes from man to man, in meeting after meeting and threads through countless conversations. For almost 50 years guys have discovered in those simple words what their Lord really wants of them.

Everything.

Like a prairie fire ignites a grassy plain, word spread across North America about Men For Missions. Dwight Ferguson, Larry Burr, Eldon Turnidge, Enloe Wallar, Stanley Tam, Archie Porter, and a growing, gathering number of others fueled the flames with passion straight from the heart of God. Men who want to do more than write a check or take a missionary out to dinner find their hearts stirred by the Holy Spirit and His insistence that they involve themselves in more ways than they dreamed possible.

The popularity of the new movement called Men For Missions by 1959 planted seeds in men's minds that gave rise to questions. When the cabinet met in St. Petersburg, Florida, a discussion arose among them about MFM's relationship with OMS. They pondered the beckoning idea of going independent rather than remain merely "the laymen's voice" of their parent mission. With more autonomy they could help other organizations as well, they reasoned.

Larry Burr wanted to take MFM across mission and church lines...but OMS balked, via the voice of Eugene Erny. Harry Burr, then a regional director for OMS, remembers what Erny said.

"At the end of the discussion, Dr. Erny stood to his feet and told them what MFM had meant to OMS since 1954, how things had changed, how missionaries felt there was someone behind them, what it meant to have MFM as part of the OMS team, and how dedication increased in their ranks because of laymen giving time and funds to help missionaries with their tasks.

"It has touched the morale of our missionaries across the world until it's at the highest point we've ever had," Burr quotes Erny. "We're seeing tremendous things happen that we've never seen before."

Erny understood what some in MFM wanted to do as an independent organization, to stimulate people affiliated to other agencies, other denominations, meanwhile continuing to help OMS.

"You may want to go and help other organizations," Erny said. "You're free to do that. We can't hold you. But MFM is part of OMS. So if you go..." he meant the men around the table..."that's okay, but *Men For Missions stays*. Think about it. Pray about it." The men thought, prayed, discussed—Harry among them—and they wept in repentance that they had even thought about pulling away from the mission. When they returned to their cabinet meeting and to Dr. Erny, they said, "We're with you. We realize this was a mistake. We will always be a part of OMS."

Chapter Four

1960s: The Haiti Connection

Men For Missions may have stayed with OMS, but Larry Burr responded to World Vision's recruiting efforts and transferred his talents to that well-known and effective international evangelism/social aid agency founded by Bob Pierce. World Vision leaders wanted him to work with lay people, something they obviously knew he did extremely well. Before he left, however, Larry recommended to OMS that his brother Harry step into MFM leadership in his place.

The brothers talked it over. "Do you really think I should do this?" Harry asked.

"Yes, I think you should." Larry was confident of his brother's skills.

Harry speaks of the opportunity as "an exciting move," but humbling because "my brother had been so successful. MFM had moved so fast and done so many wonderful things that I feared I was not up to the task." The Burrs accepted the offer, however, encouraged because "much prayer with many people behind us helped us begin."

According to MFM cabinet minutes from 1960, "...it was asked of Dr. Erny who the new executive secretary would be. He suggested the cabinet make a choice. Unanimously, the cabinet chose Harry Burr and presented this nominee to the OMS." Because OMS promptly ratified their choice, *ACTION* magazine ran a piece saying, "At the June cabinet meeting in Winona Lake, Indiana, Harry was put into office as the new Executive Secretary."

At that cabinet meeting, his first as the new MFM leader, Harry felt nervous and unsure of his welcome (his brother was a hard act to follow). But the Lord took care of his qualms in a most remarkable manner. Dwight Ferguson, who looked upon Harry as a son, stood at the head of the committee table to lead worship. Communion. He seized a crusty loaf of bread that lay on the table and broke it apart.

"This is my body, broken for you."

Ferguson handed half the loaf to the man on his right, the other half to the man on his left. Each wrested a piece from the bread and passed the remainder on to the man beside him.

"Do it in remembrance of me."

Tears coursed down weather-beaten cheeks, trickling past mouths accustomed to barking orders. Their recognition that the Savior stood among them put every fear, every agenda item, and every priority into perspective. Sure, they had the world on their hearts but they knew they couldn't move a step from that room without the empowering Master who redeemed them with the broken body and shed blood they honored that day. If He said go, go they would, straight down to the gates of hell, if sent.

Harry's nervousness evaporated and, filled with the power of the Holy Spirit as were 11 of the first disciples in the presence of the Master, he moved forward into the responsibility set before him full of peace, joy and steadfast commitment that never, ever wavered across the decades that he led MFM.

Burrs moved from their second OMS assignment to the regional office in Atlanta, and settled quickly into their niches at OMS headquarters in Los Angeles. Eleanor maintained responsibility for *ACTION* magazine (she'd presided over its birth while serving as Larry's secretary in Winona Lake) and Flo Rickards stayed at her secretarial desk, exchanging one Burr boss for another.

The 1960 MFM budget was $10,000, and at the November cabinet meeting they made plans for the future.

Harry proposed that his beginning salvo as leader should be to contact every person who had signed on for participation in MFM...about 2000 of them.

"I felt we had to know who we were working with, how many stood with us," he says. "That was our beginning in 1960."

"I sensed the encouragement of much prayer," Harry remembers. His letter went out to the 2000 but "we found only 300 or so willing to pull with us." Undaunted, Harry zeroed in on the 300, asking God for ways to involve more men, to accomplish more. And then he came up with what signaled decades of groundbreaking ideas to get the job done, a trademark of his leadership.

"While praying, I was reminded that in the Navy, for every one of us sailors out there, ten people back home were doing a job for our country. God said to me, 'Why don't you get ten lay people behind every missionary?'"

This became Harry's challenge whenever he personally talked with or spoke publicly to lay people about missions: choose a missionary, he said, and pray for her or him; become part of that missionary's support team before the Lord.

Prayer was a foundational MFM tenet from the outset. Allusions to prayer appear regularly in reports, minutes, articles, and letters. Prayer for overseas missionaries and their work characterizes council meetings and the focus of each man who agrees to go wherever God wants him to, give whatever God wants him to, and do whatever God wants him to. More often than not, what the Lord wants a guy to do, first and foremost, is pray. So he prays, and the praying usually transforms his life forever. An event, also soaked in prayer back in 1954, the year of MFM's birth, set in motion action and opportunities that would shape its character for all times.

Colombia missionary Bill Gillam learned about Spanish language gospel broadcasts coming out of Haiti that were stimulating conversions to Christ among Colombians. He began asking the Lord to let him learn where the broadcasts were coming from and why. Early that year he went to Haiti and searched out Radio 4VEH in Cap Haitien. There a band of missionaries broadcasted in several languages, including Spanish. And, he learned that the station was for sale.

At Bill's instigation, in 1958 (some things take a while to come to pass) he led a delegation back to Haiti to survey the possibilities for OMS. Eldon Turnidge, OMS board member and MFM president, was part of the group, as were singing evangelist Byron Crouse, a high school student named

David Graffenberger, and radio engineer Clarence Moore. God rounded out the delegation by guiding Harry and Eleanor Burr home through Haiti from a trip across South America for their initial exposure to missionary work.

Bottom line? The OMS board voted to add Haiti to the roster of nations where they minister. And MFMer Ray King of Hesston, Kansas, promised the $10,000 purchase price.

In 1959, the missionaries, Haitian co-workers, and MFM crusaders (tour group from North America) dedicated a new transmitter site for 4VEH. The visitors provided music and testified to God's grace through a Haitian translator. Dwight Ferguson preached and, ever the evangelist, invited those listening to ask Jesus into their lives. Some dozen or so Haitians accepted the Lord as Savior, including the man who became foreman of the transmitter project.

Then the OMS leaders took a most remarkable and innovative step by asking layman Eldon Turnidge to direct their new work in Haiti, creating a major upheaval in the life of the farmer family from the Northwest. Rachael Picazo quotes *ACTION* magazine.

"In June 1959, Eldon Turnidge and his family took another big step in their dedication and have now established residence in Haiti, where Eldon has been appointed Field Director for the MFM project, Radio Station 4VEH, and all missionary activity of the OMS on that island. Eldon is the first self-supported lay missionary ever to direct an overseas missionary work (for OMS). He also holds the distinction of being the first layman to serve on the Board of Directors of The Oriental Missionary Society and the first president of Men For Missions International. (Not entirely accurate because Turnidge succeeded the short term of Lloyd Gallimore.)

"Little did they dream," the article continues, "when they made their first trembling attempts to tell the story of Christ through an interpreter, that someday God would call them from their peppermint farm to go to a foreign country as missionaries, while being sustained by their own agricultural enterprises at home."

Bill Gillam's official letter of appointment to Eldon expressed confidence that "the field will benefit richly by your direct supervision of the work." Gillam pledged, "We shall serve you faithfully at the headquarters office."

Eldon answered Gillam's letter late one evening in July during harvest on his Oregon farm. "I'm feeling the responsibility of Haiti more and more each day, and while I shudder, I am praising the Lord for the marvelous opportunity to serve Him. My constant prayer is that the Lord will be able to find something He can use in this old stick."

And Harry Burr, in the midst of his own giant steps of faith-based change, took time to write Eldon and express his joy.

"Just wanted to let you know, fella," he wrote in August 1960, "that we are really thrilled with the possibility of your move to Haiti, and trust that things are shaping up for you in a miraculous way. You and Mary are a great blessing and challenge to all of us, and we surely appreciate your willingness to leave all and 'follow Him.' We know the Lord has even greater things in store for you, and we know that the Haiti field needs you desperately."

One individual did *not* share in the general rejoicing swirling around Mary and Eldon, however. Their teenaged son John remembers "Dad sitting me down and telling me that we were going to Haiti for the winter and that I would be going to school there. I had just been elected president of the Junior High Student Council at Salem (Oregon) Academy, as an eighth grader was playing football, enjoying the girls, and didn't want my world changed. My response to Dad was, 'Great. Have a good time. I'm not going.'

"My folks, however, were 'those kind of folks,' and I went! But I didn't like it...I was the only student in my grade level and I felt pretty lonely. I learned a lot of things like shooting bats with slingshots under missionary houses, eating mangos, killing snakes and listening to voodoo drums. My attitude was far from positive and I created some difficult times for my folks.

"I remember when we arrived and I walked into what was to be my bedroom. I took a step through the door and fell through the floor that had been eaten out by termites. If I could have flown, I would have left right then.

"During that year my mother's father, Grandpa Archer, passed away unexpectedly. Mom and Dad went back to the States for the funeral and I had to stay in Haiti, sleeping in the trailer house (imported by the Turnidges) by myself. I almost died of fear the first night they were gone when the voodoo drums beat all night long just a few hundred feet from my bedroom.

"I made it through that year and looked forward to returning to the farm that summer to work. I just wanted to get back to the States and hoped my folks wouldn't return the following year. Well, that hope was soon squelched when again I had a 'sit-down talk' with Dad. They were going back and I was going with them! I argued once more that I ought to stay in the States with grandparents or someone else so I could get 'a good education.' That didn't work. Again...I went.

"That school year, ninth grade, I did some work by correspondence. The wife of an executive in the United Fruit Company taught other subjects, such as Spanish, history, English and some literature. I had to ride a small motorbike or a horse to Cap Haitien to attend the classes, seven miles to Cap and seven back. I didn't really enjoy it. I was the brunt of racial slurs; little kids threw sticks and stones at me. Others sicced their dogs on me, and I wrecked the bike a couple of times.

"The first part of that school year was hard, discouraging and, to put it mildly, I hated being there. This was obvious and I know Mom and Dad were praying for me. I am sure they questioned their decision to go to Haiti many times because of my attitude.

"Somewhere during that school year, however, I began to see why they had left all they had, why they decided to go to Haiti. I saw the need there. An earthquake, a robbery, police brutality aren't very spiritual events but they impressed on me the need for people to know the Lord. As a result, my attitude changed. I began to learn from my time in that country, and I enjoyed being there!

"No, I wasn't a happy camper that first year and a half, but through that time in Haiti and the testimony and commitment of my folks, I was called to be a missionary."

In response to their faithfulness, the Lord transformed Mary and Eldon's rebellious son John into one of His sent ones. John and wife Dianne serve as missionaries in Spain.

A bond developed between Men For Missions and the OMS missionary work in Haiti that remains these 50 years later. A relationship created by God enabled thousands of men and women not only to visit a mission field but also to work side by side with missionary personnel and their Haitian co-workers. MFMers learned firsthand the needs of the on-site team, of the radio station, the clinic, the vocational Bible school and the churches that sprang up in the wake of evangelism efforts. Not only did they learn, but also took practical action to help whenever possible.

Harry's 1960 letter to Eldon illustrates this. "Louis Latham turned a very nice folding organ over to us for Haiti. A lady had donated it for that purpose. Dr. Fred Marget has also contacted us regarding medical instruments and medicine. He has a supply he wants to donate, and will also try to get any things that are needed....These things, along with the organ, and some pillows will be here to be taken down with whoever is going next. We also had a mike repaired which Mardy (Picazo) sent up with the PC (prayer circle) ladies, and wanted returned to Haiti...."

This useful trickle in 1960 became a river of benevolence and blessing over the decades to come, and Archie Porter explains one of the practical reasons why.

"Haiti is so close to our (North America's) own shores. We can go there for $250 (true in the 60s). It broke our hearts and gave us a world vision."

Even though Haiti lies close to American shores, transporting the material results of some laymen's wide-open eyes and sensitive hearts turned into a logistical challenge second to none. The starting place of this, according to *ACTION* magazine's 1969 article titled "Cargo for Christ," was in "the hearts of scores of MFMI crusaders who had seen the tremendous needs in Haiti and realized they could help."

What specifically did they see? Water shortage. The need for a power plant and phone system. Lack of farm equipment. Poorly equipped schools. A clinic without enough medicine. Transportation problems. And they'd already donated money for a new radio transmitter for Station 4VEH.

"Lay missionary Dave Graffenberger...became concerned (the same Dave who visited Haiti as a teenager). And, everywhere he traveled (on furlough) he found people wanting to send needed items to Haiti." Pennsylvania funded electrical equipment. Indiana rounded up beds for the clinic, desks for the school, furniture for missionaries. Iowa, Oregon, Montana, Georgia and others accumulated cars, tractors, farm equipment, drums of medicine, seed corn, clothing, sewing machines, drill presses—tons of equipment and supplies.

"There was only one answer!" the article continues. "A freighter must be chartered and trucks routed from all directions to converge in Miami on a specified shipping date. Dave, Harry Burr, and others went to work. As a result, six semi-trailers and two tandem trucks were rented or borrowed. Some 15 men volunteered to drive; a schedule of pickups was arranged. Other men were secured to load at various stops as well as Miami, and a deadline was set.

"Over the Christmas and New Year's holidays, crews of men all across the country forgot about personal plans and usual festivities. In freezing rain and snowstorms they crated, packed, and loaded their love gifts for Haiti. Then novice drivers set out, some on slippery highways, driving long hours to meet the schedule."

Troubles arose: one truck overturned on icy pavement; a Pennsylvania driver was stopped because of an "overloaded axle." But, "in Miami on January 2, arriving truckers were greeted by Dave Graffenberger, Harry Burr, and the Haiti work crusaders (30 men giving from two weeks to a month at their own expense to put the new equipment into operation, build a reservoir and tackle many other projects in Haiti). MFMers wintering in Florida also joined the group. And one, just recovering from surgery flew down from Indiana to lend a hand.

"Loading cargo was a new experience for many, and long-forgotten muscles painfully announced their presence. But never was pain more pleasant, nor work more rewarding.

"The 200-ton freighter, radio transmitter and all, headed for Haiti on January 6. A few days later word reached MFMI headquarters. By special permission from President Duvalier, the entire shipment would enter Haiti duty free.

"Reason for elation?

"The best part of 'Cargo for Christ' is yet to be written. What the Holy Spirit intends to accomplish through it in Haiti will make interesting reading indeed."

Dave Graffenberger sums up the MFM/Haiti relationship: "We (OMS) wouldn't be in Haiti if it weren't for MFM. They raised the money to begin OMS work there...their coming took Christ to the people."

Dwight Ferguson's book, *Men Plus God,* describes in colorful detail this unique event, which took place at the end of 1968, the God-fired result of Men For Missions' innovative crusade program. "Crusade" is a term cheerfully used by Christian Americans, Billy Graham included, to describe efforts to advance Christ's cause, seemingly unaware that the word heats the blood with anger in the Muslim world. Their terminology would be remedied eventually, but meanwhile MFM crusades, especially to Haiti, took off like an eagle seeking the sun. Haiti missionary Mardy Picazo describes the phenomenon from his on-site vantage point.

The Picazo family lived for years in Cap Haitien, Mardy wrote, in a house "that had been most attractive to termites. They had eaten so much of the building that I felt sure the house stayed up because teams of termites held hands while others were busy eating!

"OMS sent a survey crew to evaluate the buildings and see what could be done....It was decided new residences would need to be built and not to repair more than was absolutely necessary while new homes were being con-structed.

"The ones who undertook the first major project of construction were the laymen of OMS, Men For Missions. (Specifically Harold Harrison, a first-rate contractor, with other guys raised the funds and did the work.) They chal-lenged these men to go to Haiti and build what was needed. Soon the crusades to Haiti were top billing in the MFM ranks throughout the United States."

Lay people, men and women, poured into Haiti, a steady stream of helpers, fixers, doers, and tellers of God's good news. "The MFM crusades became a regular part of the mission's activities. The group would work on various projects during the day and at night go out with the nationals (Haitians) and missionaries to outstations for a witnessing time."

Other crusades came mainly to evangelize and witness. MFM, across the years according to Picazo, became "an important factor in the development of the radio station, the Bible school, medical center, schools, churches and other projects.... Thousands have come to the knowledge of Jesus Christ as Savior through their evangelistic tours on the fields and indirectly through the various ministries they have helped.

Larry Burr, Harry's predecessor in MFM leadership, defined the MFM crusade activity by saying, "This is a movement of the Holy Spirit who inspired the man who commits himself to a new direction...to vision for the (spiritually) lost, the whole world, not just his own community."

Such assistance was not for Haiti alone. Once the momentum built, every country where OMS fielded missionary teams—in Latin America, Asia and Europe—reaped the benefits and blessings of the visits, the prayers and the professional skills of Christian lay men and women.

Haiti equates "mission field" for countless people who can't seem to escape what they see and feel when there. Like Harry Naylor. An early participant in MFM crusades, he sat one day in a Haitian brush arbor church, watching as they took an offering. Ordinary enough, right?

Wrong.

The believers in that place were straining toward a $119 goal to pay for a concrete floor for their sanctuary. When the offering basket went round a second time, the Haitian farmer sitting behind Naylor had nothing more to give—except his well-worn straw hat, which he laid atop the basket.

Intrigued, Naylor later asked the pastor, "What can you do with that old hat?"

"Oh, we'll sell it," he said, "...maybe get four cents toward our new floor."

Then the Lord whispered to Naylor: "You buy that hat and take it back to the States." An *ACTION* article finishes the story.

"Harry handed the pastor $20, brought the hat home and began telling people about it." The first man he told "wrote a $1000 check and gave it for Haiti."

Naylor, whenever he told the story would say, "If one of you has $5000 and wants to buy the hat, I'll take your money—but I keep the hat."

That one MFM crusader, a businessman from Tennessee in the U.S., raised thousands of dollars for perhaps the neediest country in the Western hemisphere through the medium of a tattered old hat and bold, imaginative obedience to a personal, private nudge from his Lord.

Harry Naylor is in heaven now but Harry Burr has the hat. He continues to tell its story, with amazing response from challenged listeners. Imagine that Haitian farmer's surprise when he learns that heaven's ledger shows his four-cent hat is valued at well over a million dollars.

Chapter Five

1960s: Stalwarts

Harry Burr's mind churns out ideas like a fast press produces the daily news. The months were rolling on in 1963 and he knew that Men For Missions' tenth anniversary—1954 to 1964—had to be celebrated with all the flourish, gusto and excitement he could muster. MFM day at OMS convention, an instant success, always drew people who wanted to share the fellowship and to hear Dwight Ferguson's dynamic and insightful Bible studies. And perhaps best of all, listen to the guys tell how a visit to a mission field broke open their hearts and changed their lives.

So Harry pondered how to incorporate these proven features and add enough fresh challenge and incentive to draw in the curious, the unconvinced, the hungry of heart.

An anniversary extravaganza could be the perfect event to which to invite them. Even though MFM's office team functioned on overload—too much work, too few hands, too little time—Harry, Eleanor and Flo made a formidable combination when it came to special events. And they gave MFM's tenth anniversary celebration their best shot.

In 1964, *ACTION* ran a report of anniversary events in a ten-year review entitled "Decade of Dedication." Since the piece appears without a byline, Eleanor Burr, *ACTION* editor, probably wrote it herself, but without attribution. She preferred to maintain a low profile, doing her editorial best without calling attention to herself.

The article begins with a short review of how Men For Missions came into being and how men under the influence of the Holy Spirit learned to look beyond their own neighborhoods to the spiritually hungry around the world.

"Each year new faces appeared at Winona Lake... Men who had experienced changed lives as a result of a missions exposure desired to become more involved. They inspired others until this year—the tenth anniversary of that tiny beginning, the executive secretary's report (that's Harry Burr) revealed a membership of 7,850, with councils organized *internationally* (italics added) totaling 158. Greater than these statistics, however, was the impressive list of accomplishments and contributions which laymen have made to global mission."

All this, incidentally, was not limited to the United States. Canadians W.L. and Beulah Smith ignited a torch there that flamed up in laymen's hearts and sent them out across the world. Encouraged by MFM happenings in Canada, Harry went to the United Kingdom where the Irish initially seized on and implemented the idea. A trip to New Zealand and Australia accompanied by American MFMers came up with the same results. MFM became truly international, a fact that influences everything they do.

The *ACTION* report goes on to describe Men For Mission's day at the convention. "As the breakfast rally opened at 7:15 a.m., Mr. Kim (businessman from Korea) offered a prayer which although in Korean, transported the entire group to the heavenly throne. The Houghton College Trumpeters, soloist and organist from Haiti Radio 4VEH Aldean Saufley, and the bilingual Rainbow Trio (which included two Enloe Wallar daughters) now preparing to use their talents in the Colombia-Ecuador Crusade, unwrapped a musical package that delighted sensitivities, both musical and spiritual.

"In his masterful manner, Dr. Dwight Ferguson handled the roving mike, captivating the crowd with impromptu interviews from some whose missions 'injection' had been very effective. The concern for needs around the world and the realization that all could have a part in meeting the needs were indeed stimulating.

"Reluctantly the crowd moved from the cafeteria to the main auditorium, only to find there was even more to come. As various businessmen gave their pointed, practical testimonies, the Holy Spirit moved from heart to heart, nudging them to new commitment and zeal.

"Nearly 200 men gathered at the Westminster Hotel for the annual MFM luncheon. In the short business meeting it was voted to adopt over $35,000 in projects covering six mission fields from Haiti, near the shores of Miami, to half way around the world, India. Approximately $8,500 was given or pledged toward these projects....

"At 5:00 p.m., all MFM Crusaders queued along a sumptuous buffet—the second annual Crusade Club dinner. In a kinship known only among fellow team members, they reviewed crusade experiences and renewed unshakable convictions. Tears and laughter intermingled as missionaries, garbed in native dress, expressed what the Crusades have meant to their fields....

"The auditorium was filled for the closing rally, which was opened by a men's chorus in a spine-tingling rendition of the theme song, 'Militant Men for Jesus' (written by OMS VP Bill Gillam). Not a moment was wasted as one by one some of those militant men stepped to the microphone to give their account of personal and spiritual fulfillment through global Gospel involvement. Dick Capin, layman newly elected as OMS treasurer, climaxed the day with a challenge for renewed dedication.

"As one MFMer wrote after returning home, 'New desires, new decisions, and new determinations have not faded since leaving the aura of the convention and I pray they never will. My prayer life so far has been enriched, as well as other areas of my spiritual and emotional life. It doesn't cost to go—it pays.'"

OMS President Eugene Erny, who had planted world-sized seeds in Dwight Ferguson's reluctant heart, who had stood with the first batch of men under that tree in Indiana, and who had confronted the MFM cabinet with his firm conviction that MFM must stay with OMS, wrote in *ACTION* of his own thoughts about the ten-year-old "laymen's voice of OMS." He said, in part:

"I sincerely believe that the greatest contribution that Men For Missions has made to The Oriental Missionary Society and to the cause of Christ is a spiritual contribution. Men For Missions has made a spiritual thrust that has stirred the whole Society. We are grateful that at every conference we hold, the enriching spiritual atmosphere is felt when you,

Men For Missions, are there. When your banquets are over there is a spiritual uplift. We are thankful that when these crusades go to the fields they are not just trips to take pictures. Crusaders come back with broken hearts—men with passion, men with changed lives, and men who give their time and money to missions.

"In behalf of the OMS, and in behalf of the Lord, I want to express our deep appreciation for your prayers, for the spiritual contribution which you have made. If you continue on as you have, the Lord will continue to use you in material things and there will be more buildings, more dedicated lives, and advance on many fronts. I want to say, 'Thank you in the name of the Lord.'"

From the initial encounter between Erny and Ferguson, Eldon Turnidge's commitment, on through Stanley Tam's pilgrimage and Harry Burr's journey as well, clearly the Holy Spirit called the shots. Each transformation, each surrender had come, not from a charitable impulse or momentary inclination to do good, but from desire to obey God, from a heart overflowing with love for Him. Inevitably this meant that care and compassion would pour forth wherever each Spirit-led man set his foot. Then do-go-give became automatic, the only possible response to the powerful presence of the Holy Spirit. As missionary Dale McClain,

MFM's earliest expeditor said, "It isn't an organization. It is a movement of God's Spirit. It doesn't have members, there is no book of rules, there are no dues. Primarily, it is concerned with giving laymen an actual personal exposure to missions. Then, they draw their own conclusions, set their own goals, participate as God lays it on their hearts."

That irresistible holy presence produced a collection of stalwarts for MFM and OMS whose contribution to initiating gospel communication and participation cannot be overemphasized. One of the earliest of these came in response to an overload of blessing and opportunity springing up in Men For Missions. Consider these circumstances.

One of Harry Burr's most significant characteristics, one with which he served Men For Missions most effectively and thereby helped it to grow, is his ability to connect personally with man after man after man. In this he resembles—and perhaps outstrips—his mentor, Dwight Ferguson, who wrote the book on personal encounters. Just ask Stanley Tam or Archie Porter.

Harry has a further gift in that he is a skilled administrator who knows how to organize and operate an office, how to keep communication flowing, how to motivate and utilize staff. And he knows how to sell.

But as the scope of MFM grew, as more and more people signed up for mission field exposure, as guys brought their questions about service or prayer or just wanted to stand close to the man who had alerted them to the world's spiritual needs, Harry Burr found that neither his days nor his nights were long enough. Even his prodigious amounts of physical and mental energy—not to mention his time—ran out before all the opportunities did. Harry needed help.

In the early sixties, Californian Marvin Mardock had teamed up with Burr and Dr. Vernon Hall of Oregon. A special part of their work together was to take college students on mission trips to Mexico, giving these young Christians a chance to see what goes on beyond their familiar turf and to find out if the Lord wanted them to participate in His "go ye" directive.

But after all too short a time, Mardock fell ill and had to withdraw from his Men For Missions work in order to do battle with cancer that threatened his life. OMSers and MFMers went to prayer, asking for healing for their friend and colleague. At the same time, Harry sorely missed Marv's partnership in the cause to which they both had committed themselves. He still needed help, and needed it badly.

Prayers went up. The search commenced. Surely the Lord had somewhere an energetic, broken-hearted man with a passion to see other guys assume responsibility for getting out His good news.

Surely He did.

In Hampstead, Maryland, on America's east coast, Charles Spicer, Jr. exuded all the promise and presence that comes with business success, happy marriage and great privilege. Not to mention leadership in church and community. He had heard about MFM for Larry Burr had invited him to an MFM retreat in the late 50s. A few years later he and Phyllis went to South America where OMSer Margaret Brabon talked to them about their participation in mission. Plus, Bill Gillam stayed in touch by letter with the dynamic couple whom he coveted for full-time mission involvement.

Then during their Maryland church's mission conference, the Holy Spirit's tugs took over. Charlie said to Phyllis, "God is saying something to us."

"Missions was captivating us," is how Charlie explains it in retrospect.

The end result? In 1967, Charlie and Phyllis Spicer, after unanimous acceptance by the cabinet, moved from Maryland to Indiana (OMS had moved their headquarters east) to fill MFM's newly created National Director and assistant slots. Joining the Burr-Rickards team, the Spicers helped to shoulder the burgeoning load. Charlie's responsibilities included staying in touch with the councils scattered across the country and promoting overseas trips at the same time.

Within the same time frame Ron Harrington, another businessman with a passion to obey God, along with wife Priscilla was making some life-changing choices of his own.

Harringtons lived in southern California where Ron was steadily climbing the success ladder. He and Priscilla had it all—two handsome children, affluence, prestige—and they poured back into the Lord's hands a significant percentage of their time and financial resources. But He had in mind much, much more.

Ben Pearson, telling the Harrington story in *Men Plus God,* asks the key question. "It might seem that Ron Harrington was a candidate for the ideal Christian layman of the Twentieth Century. From appearances he had taken the missionary challenge 'hook, line, and sinker.' But had he? Was 20%, 25%, 30% of his income devoted to Christian work enough? Was he fulfilling that for which God had created him and sent him into the world?"

Chairing his church's committee on missions put Ron in the mainstream of the mission world. So he and his pastor "felt they must visit the Orient to bring back a special report of how the church's money was being spent and to seek additional challenges to present to the congregation." In Hong Kong, The Oriental Missionary Society people welcomed them warmly. Not too surprisingly, Field Director Dale McClain couldn't keep quiet about his enthusiasm for Men For Missions as he showed them a city full of "such torrents and waves of humanity as they had never imagined. Most of these multitudes were without Christ." And seeing the milling crowds in Hong Kong turned Harrington's feet toward a new destination.

Why does God do what He does when He does it? How often His children ask this question, wondering at His timing, His idea of sequence. Only later—when the deed is done, when the commitment is made—can we look back and nod in understanding at how the Lord guides our pilgrimage.

Charlie Spicer and Ron Harrington lived in similar circumstances even though one faced the Atlantic Ocean and the other the Pacific. Though their professional lives didn't match, the Holy Spirit wrought similar miracles in their lives. First He taught them to obey the Lord. Then he opened their hearts to God's waiting world. After they saw the needs, He asked them a pivotal question: "What are *you* going to do about this?" Then He waited for their answers, His "still small voice" reminding them what obedience to God's call would mean, and assuring them the plusses would outweigh any possible minuses if they would step out obediently on nothing less than faith.

Harrington's six-week trip with his pastor "turned everything around," he remembers. "Yes, it changed his life," adds wife Priscilla. "We found something more important than making money."

It was quite simple, really. When Ron saw OMS work in Asia, he says, "I knew I couldn't stay in business." And once God's ball started rolling, it gathered force and speed. It was already on the move when Ron went to talk with Bill Gillam.

"You probably wonder why I'm here," Harrington began their conversation.

Gillam's famous grin spread across his face. "Oh, I already know," he claimed.

And he did. He knew that Ron was ready to turn his back on his career and lend his strength, his skills—whatever they were—to telling the name of Jesus somewhere in Asia.

Momentum gathered. The escrow business Ron ran in partnership with his father-in-law sold by the end of 1961, even as he negotiated with OMS about missionary service in Hong Kong. The Harrington family arrived in that fabled city in July, 1962, ready to oversee the construction of a new clinic, plus a mission center dedicated to evangelism, church

planting, and leadership training—OMS' three core empha-
ses.

During their years in Hong Kong, the Harringtons
made many friends, both Chinese and within the expatriate
community. Two of these friends were businessman Jimmy
Coe and his wife, Barbara, a lyric soprano. Over dinner one
evening in 1964, Ron made what he thought was an offhand
suggestion.

"Barbara, would you be willing to go to the States on
a concert tour for the benefit of missions and OMS?"

This out-of-the-blue idea stemmed from the fact that
"the building program was going slowly due to lack of
funds," Ron writes in an unpublished manuscript. "Priscilla
and I had been talking and praying a lot, asking how do you
get more money?" He'd learned to obey impulses sent by the
Holy Spirit, remarkable as some of them turned out to be.

Ron continues the story: "In typical Chinese fashion,
Jimmy answered the question for his wife very promptly with
'She will be glad to go and I will pay her way.'"

But the Spirit's nudges can take your breath away.

"Wow! What do we have here? was my thought," he
writes. He had to explain his impulse and let the Coes know
he had no authority as yet to commit OMS to the project.
"From that point we talked and did some far-out imagin-

ings," he writes, and of course, neither he nor the Coes knew what was entailed in the journey ahead.

A major block stood in the way of Barbara Coe's concert tour in the U.S. in those cold war days: She had been raised by her uncle, who edited the largest Communist newspaper in Hong Kong. So, when Ron and Barbara went to the American Embassy early in 1965 to obtain her visa, a rather unpleasant woman there rudely told them it would be impossible. Give the ward of a prominent Communist a U.S. visa? Certainly not. At Ron's persistence she did lay out for them a complicated track for obtaining "a waiver of inadmissibility," purported to be the initial obstacle to overcome.

Harrington jumped through the specified hoops in spite of the embassy staffer's hostility. "We had nothing to do but wait and pray," he writes. "Praying about what we were doing all day long, even at grace at the table." Both he and Priscilla continued preparations for Barbara's tour on faith alone, for they had no evidence that bureaucracy would come through with the crucial visa.

"It was during those hours under the weight of this visa problem which now we knew was much more serious than we had expected that I went to the bedroom to pray some more about it," he continues. "As I prayed this question stopped me short: 'What's the matter, Ronald, can't you trust Me with this one? I took care of getting you to Hong Kong. This is such a small problem compared to that one.'

"Boom! I stopped and got up saying, 'Thank you, Lord.' From there I went on with an assurance that did not waiver--not cockiness but definite, positive assurance of the leadership of the Lord.

"At this same time I shared the problems with Auntie Mun (veteran China/Hong Kong missionary) and her reply was so clear that I shall never forget it. 'Ron, if you are certain this is what God wants you to do, don't let anything stop you.'"

Like a bulldog with a beloved bone, Harrington clamped down on his difficulties and took action. He phoned his friend, Kansas State Senator Ray King, and asked him to contact Senator Frank Carlson in Washington DC. Could Carlson help them cut through the tangled bureaucratic thicket? At King's request he agreed to try and put one of his staffers on the case full time.

By now, Harringtons were both in the U.S. working on Barbara Coe's concert tour and all the details pertaining to it. If this effort was to win friends to help fund the Hong Kong missionary project, it all must be done thoroughly and well. Their faith and determination shone through an encounter Ron had with Eugene Erny in the hall of OMS headquarters.

"One day," he writes, "Dr. Erny passed me in the hall of the headquarters building and said, 'Ron, what if you do not get the waiver for Mrs. Coe?' My reply was, 'Dr. Erny, it is not *what if* but *when.*'"

Concerts were scheduled up and down the American west coast when Senator Carlson phoned from the capital to say he was "at the end of his rope. If you want anything more you'll have to come to Washington to get it."

All right. In California Harrington dropped everything and worked out a travel schedule with Ray King in Kansas to go to Carlson's office. Not as easy as it sounds. Mechanical difficulties and a blizzard sought to thwart their purposes but the two men would not be denied. Hired cars and chartered planes coupled with plenty of plain and fancy persuasion got them from California and Kansas to their destination with maybe two hours to spare before their appointment on Capitol Hill. Carlson's work on their behalf plus his useful contacts finally cleared the deck and Ron's unshakable faith proved fruitful. Barbara Coe's visa came through. Ron sums up this saga of faith and tenacity:

"The first singing engagement for Barbara Coe on this tour was at an Easter sunrise service in California's Rose

Bowl before some 5000 people. Have I given enough evidence that God has men everywhere to be used if we will be used for His glory and not our own?"

He figures that Barbara Coe perhaps ministered to 25,000 people. Now the doors of the OMS center in Hong Kong's Shek Kip Mei district and Men For Mission's most ambitious project to that point swing open for students, pastors, and lay people seven days a week. From the top of the building the Christian cross shines like a beacon in the world's most densely populated city.

At the end of Harrington's Hong Kong tour as he weighed and prayed over what to do next, Eugene Erny wrote to say, "If you come to the U.S. to work, you will establish a department of development for OMS."

OK, Ron thought, looks like the decision is already made. At that the Harringtons applied themselves to a new mission challenge, several of them, in fact, over the next few years. And eventually MFM again figured significantly in their ministry.

The Oriental Missionary Society (which, because of the widening scope of its ministry, changed its name to just OMS International in the sixties) benefitted greatly from the obedience to the Lord's directives of the Spicers and the Harringtons. Both couples, gifted lay Christians, put their talents to work, not only as members of the MFM staff but subsequently in several key posts as well in OMS's world-wide ministry. As did Dick and Jeanne Capin, whose story resembles that of Spicers and Harringtons, when it comes to responding to the signals of God's Spirit.

The Capins grew up in Mt. Carmel, Illinois, the base of Dick's accounting firm, although business ventures took them to Texas for some years. Capin's expertise as a CPA gained the attention of corporate achievers who wanted to put it to work for them in exchange for what they assured him would be wealth beyond imagining.

But Dick and Jeanne had decided to follow God's leadership in their lives rather than making business success and affluence their goals. Jeanne's mother attended the Wallars' MFM/OMS prayer group, and Enloe Wallar's constant talk about his discoveries stimulated by Men For Missions plus his concern that people in other countries accept Christ as Savior, stirred their interest. Did the Lord want them to get involved?

On a business trip, Dick pondered his situation and prayed as he paced the streets of Manhattan late one night, "God, if you have anything for me more than this, let me know."

This came after his trip abroad. He and his pastor had set out across the world to learn about missions firsthand, and Dick Capin came home with a burning hunger to share his faith with men and women who know nothing about the Lord Jesus. That fire refused to die.

They, too, visited OMS work in Hong Kong, then under the supervision of the irrepressible Dale McClain. In Pearson's *Men Plus God,* Dale tells what happened during Dick's visit: "He told our Chinese friends how God had involved him in something we call Men For Missions International. It was easy to see that Dick was deeply concerned-- in heart, soul, finance, life, energy, and the very stream of his being--with trying to get out the witness of Jesus Christ. Actually, that trip nailed down some things in Dick's heart from which he's never recovered. Seeds were sown that are now producing harvest scenes, and ultimately projected Dick into another career."

Here's how it happened.

Upon Capin's return from his New York trip, he heard the phone ringing in the house as he stepped from the car. Jeanne called out to him. "Quick! You have a phone call. It's OMS. They want to talk with you."

When Dick picked up the phone, he learned that, just as he suspected, God *did* have something more in mind for him than climbing corporate ladders and amassing the rewards that such ascents can generate. He learned via the voices of MFM Director Harry Burr and OMS Vice President Bill Gillam that the mission wanted him to do some bookkeeping for them. Overseas. Would he go to Korea, Hong Kong, Taiwan and Japan to organize and systematize bookkeeping methods and financial record-keeping among these countries?

In response, Capin had only one question: "Will you let me share my witness with the world?" The inequity of opportunities suffered by so many people to learn about his Redeemer had broken his heart. Pearson writes:

"There was one condition which Dick requested--that the tasks assigned him in business administration, bookkeeping, field treasurer responsibilities and office work should never prohibit him from a personal witness. For him this was first priority. He saw the task of administration only as providing opportunities for him to offer his Christian witness in the land of Korea. To this the mission gladly agreed."

The Capin family extricated themselves from business, house, schools and stateside obligations, as God prepared their way with prayer and financial support partners. In 1961 Seoul, Korea, became their new base of operations. The OMS missionary team in Korea drew Dick and Jeanne, Sherrill and Greg into their circle, delighted to know that an expert was going to handle some of the mission's administrative duties, which Dick did easily, given his superb training and wide business experience. And through his friendship with men on the OMS staff and then with Mr. Kim, WonChul, the American accountant began to travel across Korea. As he told what Jesus means to him, Korean laymen became inspired to get involved in evangelism on their own. Men For Missions councils soon outnumbered those in the U.S. and Canada. The same thing happened elsewhere as Capin went about his OMS assignment in other countries, obeying God's directive to him to share his witness with the spiritually neglected he saw everywhere.

As Dick Capin looks back across those years in retrospect, he says, "I found something better than money...the only thing that seemed to add up."

And when the Capins fulfilled their two-year assignment in Asia, again OMS wanted Dick's expertise, this time as mission treasurer at headquarters. The story goes on and on through Capin's stepping up to demanding jobs and consulting opportunities on countless issues and projects through the next 40 years. The story continues well into the twenty-first century as the businessman with the burning heart calmly, quietly commits his gifts and his love for the world into the Master's hands.

Chapter Six

70s: Growth and Glory

Kent squinted against the rising sun as he drove east toward Iowa and home. The road running ahead of him straight as a string required little thought, leaving him free to remember and relish the days he'd spent with his family in the Rocky Mountains of western Colorado. At a missions conference, no less. Funny thing for a teenager to get excited about...but he did. The whole conference had been super great, but in the eyes of this tow-headed boy turning man, the MFM guys stood out like the grain elevators on the plains through which he passed.

"They are so cool! I want to be like them."

He discussed it with a few equally impressed friends who had also been there. They compared at length the skills and attributes of Harry Burr, Tom Gold, Howard Young, and others. What men these were! Full of energy and personality, with goals all figured out, called by God and faithful to that call. Leaders who made following pure joy.

Kent's dad seemed to think so, too. "My dad was involved in the MFM council," Kent remembers, "which meant to me it must be worth looking into...and we always had missionaries staying in our home.

"I was impressed by the men I knew who were involved in MFM....They were well respected in our community and church, as well as being successful businessmen and farmers. I looked up to these guys as men who did something, not just here at home but for missions around the world. They did projects, and they went to the field and came back and shared about it—if things needed done they did it, whether in giving or going. I also liked going to conference and being at MFM night. I was always impressed by the speaker...a layman used by God who showed me I could maybe do the same thing.

"They were my heroes," Kent says, looking back. "I even liked their orange polyester blazers. They seem funny now but looked good then."

They did stand out, those jackets. Real, true Home Depot orange. All the staffers wore them during conferences and in meetings, with black trousers and ties, or in summer with white pants, shirts and shoes. Even Dwight Ferguson sported this unique uniform and obviously enjoyed being one of the "MFM boys."

"We looked like recreation directors on a cruise ship," one staffer said, apparently less than enthusiastic about that particular idea.

Harry and Howard Young came up with the inspiration on the road one day while they brainstormed away the miles, talking about ways to make the Men For Missions image more sharp and attractive. And Kent, Kent Eller, who liked the orange jackets just fine, was destined to show up again and again on the MFM screen until the day came when he became one of the men making things happen, just like the guys he admired as a boy.

Howard Young joined the MFM team early in the seventies when Charlie Spicer accepted an invitation from then OMS President Wesley Duewel to help the mission with development matters.

Howard, an executive with Best Lock Company, had heard about the laymen's organization from his brother-in-law, Gene Bertolet, who urged him to learn what it was all about on one of their mission field ventures. Haiti's spiritual and economic needs grabbed hold of Young's heart and wouldn't let go. Actually, this awareness came as no big surprise because Howard, a man immersed in God's Word, had been praying as he read, "Do You want us to do something...for You?"

Looking back, Howard jokes, "I was praying, 'Here am I, Lord, send Jackie.'"

By which he means that following his own mission trip overseas he knew they needed unity of heart and mind if he and his wife were to embark on full-time service for the Lord. This possibility he discussed first with Bertolet, and then in conversation with Harry Burr, made it known that he and Jackie were available to God and His world in whatever capacity He chose. Maybe help out in Texas, their home at the time, in some way?

"Nothing came of talking with Harry," Howard remembers. "No particular excitement or offers." Which was fine with this calm, competent businessman. He'd offered to do whatever he could during his free time to help with laymen. Howard probably did not know that Harry was praying fervently for full-time staff to help out. And according to the Lord's timetable, eventually Young and Burr talked again, this time by a deserted hotel swimming pool in Haiti.

"Charlie Spicer is leaving MFM to go with OMS full time. Would you like to be national director in his place?" Harry asked.

Yes, he would. If God wants him there, of course he would. Simple as that. Young was the answer to Burr's prayers. "God brought two terrific guys into the office," Harry says.

One of them was Howard Young, who joined the MFM staff in 1970 after reading his Bible, talking with his Lord, and making two trips to Haiti. During the months of disengagement from Best Lock Company and readying for their move to Indiana, Young talked with his teenaged son, Dennis, about the drop in income that the family faced. Dennis wanted to go to Asbury College in Kentucky but they wondered where the funds would come from for him to attend a private school. The issue did not seem to trouble him at all.

"The Lord will take care of it," Dennis said. Which He did.

After the Young family moved from Texas to Indiana, Harry's first assignment for Howard was to read *ACTION* magazine, all the back issues, and to ask questions about anything he didn't understand.

"This was a great learning experience," Young says, "and shows to me Harry's wisdom in his method of acquainting me with MFM."

When Howard finished his reading assignment, Harry was ready with another task for his national director. "We need to revise the council program," he said. Howard went to work reading the manual, visiting the councils, and suggesting revisions he thought might work.

Also, in 1971, God brought Kentuckian Tom Gold— Harry's other "terrific guy"—onto the staff. With personality plus, Tom set out to visit, encourage, and stimulate existing councils, as well as establish new ones in five mideastern states. Not coincidentally, Tom's extraordinary singing skills warmed and blessed banquets and meetings everywhere he went. Then in 1972 at Harry's invitation, Ron and Priscilla Harrington, now living in Oregon, took over the western states for Men For Missions.

The team set a goal of a new council every week in the U.S. and Canada. They wanted to see a total of 100; a year and a half later they'd logged in the over-the-top figure of 120 laymen's fellowships, praying and giving and going on behalf of missions.

"The councils were the backbone of MFM in the 70s," Young says. "It was so powerful."

Powerful could describe burly, blond-headed Warren Hardig from southern Illinois who came on staff to join Harrington and Gold as an additional regional representative for Men For Missions. A business executive and avid outdoorsman, Hardig looks like a fellow not to be messed with;

yet just a small amount of probing reveals a caring heart and deep love for God. Tears stand in his blue eyes as Warren talks about the first poverty-ridden Haitian he introduced to the Savior. He's obviously not afraid to cry.

How did this social-drinking, poker-playing, "good-life"-loving man become who he is now? His book, *Iron Sharpens Iron*, tells the story of the "good ole boy" whom God wanted to go and share his faith far beyond his midwestern comfort zone.

But He had to get Warren's attention first, so He set wife Velma and their pastor to praying. "The pressure was on," Hardig writes. "God was dealing with me and I knew it."

Then a desperate Warren did some praying of his own. "God, would you come into my life and live through me, so I really can be a Christian? I am utterly powerless to live this Christian life by myself."

Invited to take over Warren Hardig's heart and life, the Holy Spirit began to clean house. Habits, temper, priorities, relationships...some He rearranged and some He caused to disappear completely, all of which prepared Hardig for his initial introduction to Men For Missions.

He says in his book that when Velma decided they ought to attend an MFM banquet one Saturday night in 1969, "I was far from excited. Frankly, I had my fill of those fund-raising dinners. Even more important, this was the night for 'Gunsmoke.' I wanted to spend my evening watching Matt Dillon and Miss Kitty, not in some stuffy meeting room sandwiched between people I didn't know and would never see again."

Even as Hardig peered at his watch and wished it were time to go home, he saw that speaker Harry Burr "oozed excitement and that surprised me. Most of the banquets I had attended were dull, dull, dull." But when Burr began talking about trips for people to visit missionaries and see what they do and even help them do it, interest stirred within him. "I could see myself heading into the jungles of South America to help missionaries and build churches...It fit my macho image and would allow me to serve the Lord...Right then and there I decided to go on a crusade, little dreaming what it would set in motion."

At the end of this segment of Warren's story, he writes, "That trip to Haiti literally changed my life. I had always prided myself on being a tough, macho type, but Haiti broke my heart. Haiti is where I learned to cry. It taught me the meaning of a lost world."

Howard Young and Harry Burr, in prayer over the growth of MFM, saw that they needed another regional man to do in the center of the U.S. what Tom Gold and Ron

Harrington were doing in their sectors. "We need a man for central U.S.," they agreed.

By 1973, Warren Hardig, business executive and young Christian, leader of a large and active MFM council and feeling directed by God toward new horizons, submitted to orientation and training under Howard Young. He became a regional director, a full-time staffer. And the Lord had more, much more, planned ahead for His burly, warm-hearted son. Early in the 70s MFM grew, expanded, and developed in an impressive variety of ways, offering men a multitude of opportunities to involve themselves in world mission. These methods were practical, down-to-earth, man-sized methods to aid and abet professional missionaries on the job, ways to stretch their resources, remove rocks from their paths, and cut back on the amount of time each task required. The tried and true opportunities remained and expanded, and statistics from those days are impressive.

According to cabinet minutes, by 1970 over 2000 people had visited mission work in Asia, South America and the Caribbean.

In 1971 the regional directors on the MFM team worked on expanding councils and getting more men involved. Their purpose in this was clear: "We don't want organization for its own sake, but for a chance to relate to the men's spiritual expansion and growth," said Tom Gold.

By now Men For Missions, thanks to lay people who donated the vehicles, provided 67 cars for overseas missionaries and homeland staffers to drive, which they did to the tune of over a million miles. Cost to the OMS? Only $64,000. By 1974 the car count rose to 75.

Another project involving wheels also became part of MFM's roster early in the decade when Ken Milone, an Illinois farmer, showed his new truck to Harry Burr. According to Hardig's *Iron Sharpens Iron,* Ken said, "The only thing that bothers me is that it will sit idle for half the year. I only need it at harvest. I wish I could make it productive the rest of the year."

Burr's fertile idea bank did not fail him this time either. "Well, Ken, you could haul household goods from Greenwood to Miami or to the east or west coasts when missionaries leave for the fields."

Harry's timing was perfect—truth to tell, the timing probably belonged to God—for back in January of 1971, according to an *ACTION* article by Juanita Merrill, Milone had knelt with his roommate at an MFM retreat and prayed, "Lord, use us more fully; make us better witnesses for you."

Following that commitment prayer, Merrill writes that "Kenny was prompted (the "prompt" came from Harry Burr) to offer use of his farm truck to transport goods for missions and missionaries," and he logged 35,000 miles in "the Lord's service."

The account in *Iron Sharpens Iron* goes on to tell that Milone's willingness to minister with his truck birthed "an idea that has eliminated hundreds of thousands of dollars in shipping costs for OMS ever since. More than 30 trucks and twice as many drivers stood ready to move mission-slated freight toward its destination under Ken's coordination. Government regulations regarding such donations required, however, that MFM buy its own truck. Under the new requirement volunteers continued to deliver the goods to where they needed to be. And to ice the cake, Ken became a full-time OMS missionary in 1975.

In spite of an amplified staff, work and ministry requirements continued to pile up in the MFM office. The Lord was readying a couple of men, however, to take hold and help in a unique way. Again, as is true in so many lives, after exposure to mission work in Haiti, a couple of newly fired-up guys thought of a way they might be of assistance. In *Iron Sharpens Iron*, Wally Yoder tells how he and Buss Rassi got involved.

"It was a clear spring night in 1973 when we climbed into Buss's single-engine plane and flew from northern Indiana to MFM headquarters in Greenwood. That night we met with Howard Young, Tom Gold, and MFM Director Harry Burr."

Yoder and Rassi presented their idea of how they wanted to help MFM by talking up work crusade opportunities to new men. After all, Wally and Buss had gone to see, felt the burning touch of the Holy Spirit on their priorities, and then put their expertise to work erecting a 30,000 gallon water tank for the Haitians and missionaries the two laymen went to visit.

"Harry gave immediate approval," Yoder says, "and the 'work crusade' program was officially underway. Harry said he had been praying for additional manpower and help in bringing new inspiration and growth to Men For Missions. But he didn't expect it to come from outside the OMS staff."

The Rassi/Yoder initiative created a new way of connecting MFM staff and volunteers, a new chapter in the movement. The guys went to prayer over what to call it and when they finished, the "associate staff" was born, the beginning, Wally writes, "of a program which grew into a large contingent of volunteers—men who, with no more than a phone call, were ready to assist MFM in a number of ways."

Yoder and Rassi recruited and launched to several countries 11 work teams in their first year as MFM associate staffers; 18 the second year, 21 the third, and 28 the fourth. OMS missionaries in the more distant parts of the world, seeing what was happening for their colleagues in Latin America and the Caribbean, hungered for lay workers to come their way as well, to build, to paint, to wire, to repair...and to pray for them when they returned home.

By 1975, when Buss Rassi had to relinquish his part in the program, these volunteer associate staff men were seeing off more than 30 teams per year. Wally continued alone until 1979, meanwhile running his own iron fabricating company and using its resources to pay his astronomical phone, travel and postage bills.

And that isn't all. "Once I put the team together I felt an obligation to meet them at the airport, brief them, and make certain they got on the plane without problems. It wouldn't be right to send someone halfway across the world without some sort of personal contact and instruction. I would leave my office on Friday afternoon, fly to the port of embarkation, and send crusades off—or meet returning crusades, all weekend....Finally, pretty much exhausted, I'd head home on Sunday night," Yoder said.

No man could run a business and MFM's work team program forever without paying a price. Doing this for years affected Yoder's health and forced him to slow down until he turned over the reins, reluctantly, to a new coordinator.

"The Lord used my first trip to the mission field to open my eyes....I discovered that the work of the layman is as important as the work of the missionary; it's just a different application of effort," he reflected in *Iron Sharpens Iron*. "My advice...is to get to a field. It doesn't mean much until you see it, smell it, feel it, and experience it. It will break your heart, but if I had it to do all over again, I wouldn't change a thing."

In the MFM annual report for 1976 as published in *ACTION,* 34 work teams put in 21,141 man hours worth, at a conservative $5.50 per hour, $116,275. As regards trucking, in 11 months 178,390 pounds valued at $147,000 traveled 93,000 miles; 54 drivers paid $6,200 on their own expenses in order to help 22 mission families stay on the job.

Transportation, always an issue in missions, took yet another form in Wings For Missions coordinated by Colorado businessman and pilot, Harold Miller. He compiled a roster of private planes and pilots, volunteers on whom he could call to move missionaries and MFM staff people from Point A to Point B anywhere in the U.S., reducing their travel time and cost to a minimum.

"Field advisors" is another term that joined the MFM lexicon during the 1970s. They are mentioned in the November 1971 cabinet minutes, and then in 1974 it is noted that advisors were active for OMS work in Brazil, Haiti, and India. Harry Burr describes this effort as assembling "experts in specific areas like maintenance, office management, insurance, etc. They made advice available overseas and to homeland administrators." The idea was not to control, but when they saw needs to recommend minor changes and how they could be made. "Always field advisors would step in and fill the gap in their areas," Harry says.

In the 70s MFM launched a series of Caribbean cruises, mission conferences at sea, with Bible teaching, prayer times, good music, and mission tours in several ports including, quite naturally, Haiti. This inspiration came in response to a frequent excuse from those who said they would like to see missions firsthand but feared flying. "Let's take the mission conference to sea," was the solution.

More regional directors came on line: Bob Montague replaced the Harringtons in Washington when they moved to Indiana. Francis Muia, after lay missionary service in Haiti, stepped in for Tom Gold in Kentucky; and Jim Murray, who later took over at MFM headquarters when Howard Young shifted to the OMS post of National Ministries, then to Vice President of Administration. He and Jackie then moved to France in 1982 to open new missionary work there.

Men For Missions was on the move, improvising, growing, shifting, and seeking God's face for each opportunity. Nothing seemed too hard so long as it focused on helping men see the world with eyes of compassion and commit to doing, going, and giving as the Lord directs.

Dwight Ferguson allegedly retired at age 70, but as soon as the ceremonies ended, he and Stella began a national round of council visits so Dwight could teach MFMers about the power of the Holy Spirit. At the same time, cabinet minutes record that Enloe Wallar, Ferguson's contemporary, spoke of times in the early days of MFM "when men spent whole nights on their faces before God seeking His will." Enloe "expressed hope that we not lose this. What would it avail if we build in the flesh? We must build on the Solid Rock—Jesus."

And yet another major operation lay just ahead that would stretch Men For Missions' resources, personnel, human stamina, and spiritual strength to lengths beyond imagining, an undertaking that could never have come to pass without the power and glory of the Holy Spirit.

Warren G. Hardig
International Executive Director
1983-Present

Chapter Seven

70s: Penetration '79

At a retreat in Indiana, Dr. Robert Coleman, famed advocate and teacher of the role of evangelism in a believer's life, spoke to the OMS staff, saying simply that Christians should do all possible to take the good news to everyone in the world.

"What a burden came on my heart that morning," Harry Burr says. "At the close when everyone went to lunch, I went to the altar and started praying." Harry's burden was to get laymen to go door-to-door with the gospel as OMS missionary men had done in the 1920s. It burned on his heart.

Garnett Phillippe, former India missionary, saw Harry stay behind to pray. "What's going on, Harry?" he asked.

"I want to go to some specific country with the gospel," Burr replied. "I don't know how yet but I feel God wants us to get some men to do this."

"I'm behind you, Harry, and I'll be praying with you."

Later that same year, 1962, while leading a tour to Ecuador, Harry gave up his place on an overloaded plane to ride a local bus from Cuenca in the mountains down to the port city of Guayaquil. That ride broke his heart as he gazed at the Ecuadorians surrounding him, thousands of people who knew not his Savior. How he longed to field a battalion of laymen to witness door-to-door about Christ's love. Plans, dreams, ideas and prayers flooded his mind and heart. He could envision how it could be done, and oh, how he wanted to do it.

Ever the man of action, Burr presented his burden to the MFM cabinet at his first opportunity. The men stared back at him, sympathetic—but not too excited about the idea. Harry took his load to the OMS board. Same skeptical reaction.

"I put it on the table for a while, but I still continued to pray about it," Harry says. "About 1967 I felt led to bring it up again." Still no takers.

True to his pattern, Burr prayed on, often dragging out his file full of thoughts about how the job could be done...in Ecuador. Ever since his long, dusty bus ride and the hours of rubbing shoulders with people who didn't know his Lord,

Ecuador became the target of his dream. He honed the details in his mind and heart: Fewer than 100 men? Include Ecuadorian Christian leaders to team with North American laymen? Give a month to the job?

Years sped on but mission administration and MFM's own cabinet still didn't buy it although Burr pitched the idea with skill and passion. Back to prayer. Back to seeking God's plan for the burden that would not lift, the dream that would not die.

"During an annual goal-setting meeting of the Men For Missions cabinet," writes Lee Huffman in *Impacto! The Story of Penetration '79*, "Harry felt led of the Lord to present his vision again. This time he asked for 100 men who could march against the darkness in Ecuador for 30 days.

"To his astonishment, God seemed to open their hearts. A spirit of unity and fellowship prevailed. The machinery of mission began to move and the year of 1979 was set as a target date."

The next step, blocked until now, proved equally easy to negotiate. The OMS Board of Directors approved the plan "enthusiastically."

Huffman continues: "Doors now swung wide. A survey recruited 130 members of Men For Missions who were willing to spend 30 days in Ecuador for the purpose of calling Ecuadorians to faith in Jesus Christ."

In 1977, mission administrators asked Harry Burr to attend Ecuador's annual field council meeting, a time when the entire OMS missionary team gathers for planning, reporting, and fellowship. At the meeting he talked to the missionaries about his evangelism plan, and the wheels, to this point frozen and immobile, began to turn. The field council agreed to a team of 100 men. On the spot they divided Ecuador into three districts: Quito, Guayaquil, Loja. The men would need training about culture, some rudimentary Spanish, background reading and even a boost in fitness for the long days of walking and climbing, dealing with altitude and tropical heat. An Ecuadorian or Colombian would go door-to-door in designated neighborhoods with every three or four men, and a missionary would be on deck each evening for evangelistic meetings.

The missionary council and Harry Burr agreed on November 1979 as their starting date. Burr's evangelism file, so long relegated to the bottom of the heap in his briefcase, now lay open before him. The notes he'd made, the ideas he articulated there seemed headed for realization.

Early in 1978, however, in England Burr received a telegram from Ecuador citing second thoughts about the number of men. After all, the missionaries knew that caring for 100 foreigners would tax their ability beyond imagination to keep them fed, watered, washed, and well. They wanted to cut the number to 12, a bitter blow to Harry's long-patient heart. After all, the publicity had already gone out to MFMers, already more than 12 had signed up.

Wisely, Burr quelled his protests and went to prayer before doing anything else. Then he replied, "Let's leave it up to the Lord. If He wants 100, He'll send them. If 10, we'll have 10. Please consider."

Ecuador missionaries agreed. "So we went on from there," Harry says.

Huffman reflects in *Impacto!* about the journey that led to this place. "Fifteen years of agonizing defeat and discouragement! A decade and a half of soul struggle! Then suddenly: 'Now, my son, you have been faithful to my vision, and I am going to reward you. My blessing will be added to this task I have given you to do. It will be accomplished in its proper time.'"

Burr and company swung into action. The men studied Ecuadorian and OMS history, did their morning exercises and listened to Spanish language tapes. Harry stopped in at a Greenwood, Indiana, department store to talk to owner Lloyd Walker, newborn Christian, thanks to Burr's winsome witnessing. Walker agreed to a "greatly reduced price" for dress suits, one gray and one blue for each North American and Latino, and he "designed ties to match each outfit," Harry says. These ties "he had made and donated them to the evangelists."

During the 1979 summer OMS conferences both in Indiana and Colorado, the lay evangelists were dedicated publicly to the work that lay ahead of them. The men and women sat scattered through the audience in each venue and when the moment came, they stood and moved to the front of the auditorium singing, "I have decided to follow Jesus, I have decided to follow Jesus...no turning back. No turning back."

As they stood with bowed heads, many with trickling tears, OMS President Wesley Duewel commissioned them in the name of the Father, Son, and Holy Spirit.

ACTION magazine in February 1979 ran an article by John Newsom titled "Penetration '79 Update." After listing the disciplines they were adhering to, Newsom writes, "They are preparing for one of the greatest evangelistic opportunities in the 25-year history of Men For Missions."

Newsom goes on to tell what that evangelism opportunity will entail: "Knocking on doors, they'll present the gospel message house-to-house during the day. And in conjunction with national evangelists and believers, conduct evangelistic rallies each evening."

The preparation of the men and women from North America was not the whole story, however. "In a similar way, national Christians are being recruited for Penetration. They, too, are engaged in Bible study, as well as learning to speak English. The combined efforts of stateside laymen, nationals, and missionaries from Ecuador and Colombia are a remarkable example of the unity of the Body in a ministry to reach Ecuador for Christ."

Children's meetings in the three cities would draw kids, and their parents, into the sound of the gospel. For this, Iowan John McLaughlin would take his puppets that miraculously learned to speak Spanish somewhere along the way.

"As in all MFMI activities," Newsom writes, "Penetration crusaders will pay their own way. Each has made a large financial commitment to support this extensive project. In addition to their own expenses, they are assuming the responsibility of the national co-workers, the purchase of supplemental vehicles, and a contribution to construction of several new churches." Home churches, friends and relatives became partners in Penetration '79 with prayer and donations, backing without which they would fail.

They all arrived together on November 15th—North Americans, Colombians, Ecuadorians, a 75-member battalion to divide into three evangelism squadrons, one to Quito, Ecuador's capital, another to Guayaquil, steamy port city on the coast, and the third to Loja, nestled high in the Andes mountains.

Huffman describes in detail the business of moving the group and their prodigious mountain of luggage. The baggage included not only personal items any traveler can't seem to leave home without, but also true necessities like sleeping bags, granola bars, puppets and their props, books, cameras and--top priority--extra shoes. Plus sound equipment and medicine. All important, all utilized...especially those shoes.

Met by a cadre of OMS missionaries at Simon Bolivar Airport in Guayaquil, the 79ers sailed through customs, thanks to those missionaries and their groundwork. They "followed their luggage," Huffman writes, "through the busy terminal and out onto the sidewalk. There the missionaries had a number of vehicles waiting, but taxicabs had to be commandeered for the remaining luggage.

"The lobby of Hotel Humbolt was positively paralyzed by the influx of equipment and baggage. An extra room had to be rented, just to store the overflow where it could be safely locked up. The invasion force had landed."

Divided into three platoons, they headed for their destination cities. Two boarded flights, one south to Loja and one north to Quito. The third stayed in coastal Guayaquil.

Quito

The Quito group deplaned at 9,000 feet above sea level and immediately began working much harder for their oxygen. They discovered that a quick turn could bring on a dizzy spell and climbing a flight of stairs felt like an hour on a treadmill...in slow motion. Altitude sickness felled three of the team briefly until adjustment set in.

The Ecuador missionaries took the MFMers straight to their barracks in Quito Sur, south Quito. There they found "basic" accommodations in this shanty section of the city. Wooden bunks assembled by missionary Bill Spate and crew provided four-inch foam mattresses to protect 79er bones from the plywood "springs." The team had two bathrooms, or so they thought until one stopped functioning and the landlord never got around to fixing it during their stay.

Close by stood a small new church called Bethel, whose nucleus of believers had prayed and waited for the band of men who would help them evangelize their community.

Bill Spate had taken on the task of finding a vacant lot and building the church. With the help of Ecuadorian masons scooped up off the street where such craftsmen wait for work, the building stood complete...well, almost. On the evening of the dedication service, Spate stood on a ladder installing a ceiling light as the platoon of North Americans and Colombians walked through the door. Bethel Church, *Iglesia Betel*, was "open for business," the business of pointing Ecuadorians to the Savior.

Former Army drill sergeant Warren Hardig, who'd come a long way from Southern Illinois, coordinated the Quito contingent and, according to *Impacto!*, soon had his troops briefed and ready. Lee Huffman says, "All of us sensed that something great was going to happen in our lives. We prayed that the same thing would happen to hundreds of Ecuadorians during our sojourn among them. The plans called for opening the battle in *Quito Sur*," a suburb that had sprung up on the south side of the city.

"Its streets and sidewalks...were totally inadequate to accommodate people, animal transportation, automobiles, and trucks. Dust filled the entire area in dry weather and mud whenever it rained."

In spite of the difficulties in their surroundings, the 79ers promptly discovered the flat roof of their barracks and took to doing morning devotions there while looking out across the city to the mountains beyond. "I believe those devotional periods were some of the most memorable of my life," Huffman writes.

Missionaries organized pre-campaign publicity, plastering *Impacto '79* posters all across the region. Spanish-speaking teammates stood armed and ready to lead the North Americans into evangelistic battle. All that remained was to do it. To march up and down the dusty streets of south Quito, offering the good news that Jesus saves.

Prayer saturated all they'd done in preparation. They knew their families, the missionaries of OMS, MFMers the world over were, Huffman writes, "asking for God's anointing on us for fruitful endeavors. With prayers of this magnitude, something had to happen."

Huffman says that after prayer, private and together, the platoon received their instructions: "Warren Hardig and the missionaries handed out assignments. Two North Americans and one Colombian were named for each team. We were asked to keep strict account of each call, of the number of pieces of literature distributed, and of decisions made. The organizers wanted the names and addresses of those who showed interest but who made no confession so that additional calls could be arranged. In this manner, our sheets at the end of the campaign would show whether we had been profitable servants."

Eighteen men, Latins and North Americans, fanned out into their sectors near the newly built Bethel Church. As they approached doors one by one, the MFMers silently rattled heaven's gates behind their smiles while their South American teammates greeted the one who answered their knock.

In his book, Lee Huffman describes his first encounter. "Our team approached the first street. Henry (Duarte of Bogotá, Colombia) smiled, gave us the universal thumbs-up sign, and walked to the door of a neat little house. He paused briefly to pray, then knocked lightly. My heart was racing as if I were about to meet an international celebrity. I looked at Paul (Jones from Illinois, USA). His face was fixed, anxious.

"The door squeaked open. *'Buenos dias,'*" said a short stocky woman....As she stood in the doorway to her home, her large brown eyes carefully surveyed the three men before her.

"'*Buenos dias, Senora,*' replied Henry, smiling as he held out his hand. Handshaking is an important part of all Ecuadorian greeting. He quickly introduced himself and explained our mission. Now it was time for Paul and me to shake her hand and say good morning in Spanish....

"This little lady seemed to be thrilled that we had called on her. While we could not converse with her we could converse with the Savior. He would not only understand us, but be able to minister to that woman."

The men learned that whenever the resident invited them inside, the visit resulted in a commitment to Christ. People often exclaimed, "We have been waiting for someone like you to come and tell us this wonderful message." After such encounters the team walked away with celebration in their hearts.

"Not every day brought mountain-top experiences," Huffman acknowledges. "Satan was ever on the alert to catch us off guard."

Feelings of uselessness, of being "merely a doorstop while our Colombian brothers carried the ball," sometimes piled up. But then the balance tilted back when they heard "converted Ecuadorians say that the very presence of North Americans with the Colombians at their doorstep was important to them."

They saw Christian brotherhood, unity of purpose, and a single voice in the combination which caused them to pause and listen. "That testimony came from nearly every person who accepted the Lord," according to Huffman. "And each time we heard it our zeal was spurred anew."

Nightly meetings in Bethel Church reinforced the message of the teams navigating throughout the neighborhoods. And when gospel films or John McLaughlin's puppet show came by, the little church could not contain the crowds.

Guayaquil

"You mean these people actually live here?"

"Disbelief, sorrow, and depression" form most newcomers' first reaction to *Calle Veinte Cinco* (25th Street), a "place of thatched roofs and flimsy bamboo huts built on stilts above the tidewater flats of the Guayas River estuary. There the tides of the Pacific Ocean ebb and flow beneath 40,000 lost and weary people, carrying out to sea much of their human waste and garbage. Somehow, through the grace of God, the people survive. But filth, stench, and hopelessness are their daily lot. They feel there is no power that will elevate them from their present status." So goes Lee Huffman's impression of the neighborhood where the MFMers planned to evangelize that November in 1979.

Although warned about the situation by their leader, John Newsom, the team had not comprehended the severity of the conditions to which they must adjust. Adjust they did, though, leaning hard on their Lord and counting on Him to supply stamina, fortitude, and enough love to draw the suffering residents of the neighborhood into the family of God.

Here, too, stood a newly built church in the center of the wretched city on stilts. Pigs, dogs, roosters co-existed with human residents, and all suffered from stifling heat and humidity. The 17 evangelists slept in bunk beds in a "hot, poorly ventilated room upstairs over the kitchen. The rest-rooms were downstairs at the opposite end of the church. Little was said about the fact that water for the bathrooms was available only about four hours a day." Difficult though it was, Huffman says that complaints about the limitations and discomforts were minimal.

More to the point even than their living difficulties, the evangelists learned that the residents of the region mis-trusted the motives of anyone who claimed to want to help them. Huffman wrote, "It took patience to hold on until your love penetrated and overcame the deep-seated suspicions, fears, and superstitions bred into their lives by countless years of poverty, hopelessness, and denial to themselves and their children." But if they could bring themselves to listen and even respond, "they became new creatures in Christ."

These 79ers followed the same pattern as those in Quito. Divide into cells of three men, prepare their literature for distribution, map out a strategy for their assigned sector...and pray. North Americans, Colombians, Ecuadorians never stepped out into the grim streets without saturating themselves and their task in prayer.

And those prayers produced the guts to march into situations the likes of which they'd never seen, plus the grace to talk about their Savior with conviction and love. What difference did it all make? Lee Huffman tells about one evening's evangelistic meeting in the church on 25th Street.

"As the prayer services drew to a close, sounds from early arrivals at the gate grew in volume. The Penetration team lined up at the door for a formal greeting committee.

"It was worth all the work, money, and hardships of the whole Penetration '79 thrust to see the awe and pleasure on faces that filed between the uniformed men. Ecuadorians seemed to love the North Americans' friendly greetings, their handshakes in brotherly love, their evening greetings of *'Buenos noches.'*"

Nothing could contain their joy as the guys spotted individuals with whom they'd shared the gospel just a few hours before. "Ricardo (Colombian evangelist) and his team had just taken their seats...when they noticed the 'single' mother with her three children. She searched up and down the aisles until she spotted her new friends. Upon reaching

Ricardo she held onto his handshake, looking intently into his face. Then she drew her children around her and talked excitedly in Spanish. Later we learned that she had repeatedly thanked Ricardo and told him that each of her children wanted to accept Christ that night.

"The team's joy multiplied as two other families they visited that afternoon appeared at the service with their children. What an evening! What a thrill to see the harvest gathered in."

Harry Burr's vision was bearing spiritual fruit. A vision long delayed. Countless hours of prayer. Tenacity, trust, and finally, Ecuadorians born into the family of God.

Chapter Eight

70s: Penetration '79 Continues

Behind the scenes, Ecuador's OMS missionaries labored through the month to keep the 79ers fed, their clothes clean, their illnesses tended, their spirits lifted. Bill and Joyce Spate even took the Quito team to their home on Thanksgiving Day. "We could hardly get them to come and eat turkey," Bill says. The problem? The Spate telephone upstaged their dinner because rather than eating, the men stood in line to call home, unabashedly shedding tears of homesickness.

Missionary Roger Skinner remembers their concern over the details of caring for such a large band of visitors. As soon as they agreed to Harry's plan, questions mushroomed. First came, "Where are we going to house these people?" Excited about the church planting possibility, at the same time they wondered, "If we start a church, where is it going to be?" The third question, Skinner acknowledges, had to do "with feeding the people, and issues such as safety, laundry, hygiene, and sanitation." After all, the missionaries would be morally responsible to protect and preserve the visiting evangelists. They knew only too well what all could go wrong.

"When we selected the sites we wanted to get the Penetration people to live as close as possible to where the church would be planted. In Quito we rented a house within walking distance of the church. In Guayaquil we found no (suitable) place for them, so they had to stay in the church itself."

As Lee Huffman wrote in *Impacto!*, accommodations in Guayaquil stretched the visitors far beyond the familiar. "Probably one of the biggest challenges," Skinner admits, "was the heat in Guayaquil. Sleeping in the church was difficult, with all the animal sounds (pigs, dogs, ducks, chickens, donkeys) as well as people noise. We ended up pulling out a couple of people every day. They stayed in a missionary home for an evening to get cleaned up, to eat American food, and sleep in a room where it was cooler, maybe with an air conditioner or at least a fan running. As we cycled people through this, it helped their morale at least."

Wayne Weaver remembers this: "Oh, that was such a blessing, to get a night's rest and a shower." But good food and clean skin did not protect Weaver and two of his teammates from catching hepatitis. "I spent two months in bed with that," he says.

Regrets? Not for Wayne. "It was a neat experience for my life," he says. "God blessed me through that."

Harry Burr and Roger Skinner gave overall direction, traveling to each site once a week. "We flew to an area," Roger remembers, "spent a day or two with them and then went on to the next site and did the same thing. In that way we were able to give guidance, oversee the program, and share what was going on in other places. We could encourage them, pray with them, and get a good idea of what was taking place."

Backed by this brand of concern and support, the third 79er platoon headed for the hills, the Andes Mountains, to be precise.

Loja

Loja is home to 80,000 people who live at an altitude of 7,000 feet in mountainous southern Ecuador. In this thriving, orderly town, OMS had no work already in process, so the MFM evangelists started from scratch with their Colombian and Ecuadorian co-workers to share the story of the living Christ.

Missionary planners could not find a rental place suitable for the team so they bargained with a local hotel for a decent room-and-board price for the men. What they settled on turned out to be quite satisfactory, especially when compared to the Guayaquil facilities, which perched on pilings out over the steamy tidewater flats.

Contrary to the other two venues, each room had its own bathroom, which three guys shared. Running water was available most of the time, and they ate in the hotel dining room. It's true they climbed five flights of stairs to their rooms, but on balance they walked a mere three blocks to the meeting place. And in Loja no nucleus of believers awaited their arrival, praying for the success of their venture. The men had to prepare a place of worship before holding meetings in it. Missionaries Marshal Cavit and Bruce Callender chose a vacant lot on the edge of a park where they roughed out a plan for a simple sanctuary.

By the end of their first day, after clambering off the plane, finding their rooms and digging out their tools, the men built a platform and pulpit. By meeting time the sound system was functioning. Never mind that no roof sheltered them as yet. Disappointment rewarded their efforts, however. Almost no one showed up for the amplified service of praise and worship; only "a few curious on-lookers," Huffman says.

After this initial setback, though, the MFMers went to prayer, along with their Colombian and Ecuadorian evangelist brothers and the missionaries. They determined to be "imitators of God...and walk in love as Christ loved us..." (Eph. 5.1).

"'This is the way it was in Loja," according to *Impacto!*, "throughout the four weeks in the harvest field. Great things happened. God's love was the common denominator."

That's not the end of the story, however. Before they could relax and look back across the month with joy and praise, the men had to march out into each day and not only knock on doors, but finish the task of building the physical church as well.

Heavy plastic sheeting supported by pipe formed the roof. Electric bulbs soon dangled from the ridgepole, aided by spotlights aimed at the pulpit. A "dry and private place to worship," Huffman calls it, "humble but attractive. The Lord was there and His presence added an indefinable beauty."

The pattern shifted after the first disappointing night. People began to fill the new sanctuary. Daytime calls paid off by stimulating interest among the people of Loja, and when John McLaughlin and his Spanish-speaking puppets came to town they filled the benches with dozens of children squirming with anticipation. Intrigued parents followed children and "eventually many came into the fold." Others even attached themselves to the evangelism teams so they too could go door-to-door, adding their witness about Jesus.

At the end of the month, the Loja 79ers closed out their campaign by tearing out the church's temporary pipe and plastic roof and installing a permanent one to leave behind. At the final service, 180 people packed the small chapel and 18 of them found salvation that night. Pastor Constante and his family stood ready to continue the ministry begun by MFM.

Lee Huffman tells about their departure. "Leaving Loja was not easy. They had learned to love many people there. The couple that owned the hotel (and whose children accepted Christ) had become like house parents to them. When they left, the surrounding hills would no longer be a source of inspiration. The almost perfect climate would be left behind for cold winter temperatures back in North America.

"Deep sighs were heard as the vans climbed the steep grades out of beautiful valleys. Some of the sighs turned to sobs as the vans topped the crest of the rim and started down the other side.

"God keep those whom we have brought to your fold. Shepherd them well, Lord. We love them, too."

On December 13, the three platoons reassembled at Hotel Humboldt in Guayaquil. Time had come to take pictures and to thank the missionaries. To vow to pray for one another. To agree together to remember and to intercede for the people to whom they'd witnessed. The men who took over shepherding duties of new believers in the three cities needed prayer as well.

The MFMers began to turn minds and hearts toward home. December was upon them, Christmas was coming and "thoughts of loved ones we hadn't seen for nearly a month began to dance in our hearts and heads."

A farewell dinner with the missionaries expressed 79er gratitude for "their unrelenting helpfulness." For clean clothes, for a haven in their homes, for translating, money exchanging and guided shopping tours.

Before boarding the plane for home, Harry Burr organized a final debriefing. Each of the three teams had 30 minutes to recount the highlights of their month of evangelism.

Guayaquil The blue-clad (or gray, according to uniform-of-the-day orders) MFM evangelists to 25th Street seemed to represent Christian brotherhood to the residents there. This fact often lay at the core of Ecuadorian decisions to follow Jesus.

When dysentery raged through their ranks, the temptation to fall back to the healing quiet of missionary homes almost overwhelmed them. "But the answer was always clear: 'My grace is sufficient; try Me.'" They stayed among their poverty-ridden, spiritually dispossessed neighbors. And because they shared the same wretched conditions, people found God.

Loja   This platoon "had a glorious report to share. They had started from scratch and built a vibrant congregation of new Christians."

The men recited the testimonies of the newly re-deemed of Loja who spoke of opened eyes and changed lives, of being touched by the unity of the North Americans. And in review, the guys found desire to do it again hovering high on their priority lists.

Quito Sur   This platoon celebrated the highest number of conversions. Eagerness to share Christ drove them through the streets. The evening meetings provided another opportunity to tell the citizens of South Quito about the Savior.

During their times together as a team, "hilarity was the keynote." They validated the belief that laughter is healthful, because only a brief bout or two of altitude sickness slowed their breakneck pace.

Then during the final moments of their farewell session, Lee Huffman described what "our beloved General

Harry Burr, along with Field Director Roger Skinner," had to say.

"It was a joy to listen to these two men, both with the unusual ability to take the Word of God, hold it up to the light, and make the truth glitter and radiate.

"Roger spoke of the seemingly impossible task which had been accomplished. He relived for us the tremors of fear and frustration by those on the field when presented with Harry's plan. How would they handle so many extra people at the already over-crowded OMS compounds? Where would they get funds for the needed building program? Every avenue of search seemed to dead-end. But even with prospects dark and unlikely, there persisted brightness, a distant gleam of light, a dawning that could not be turned off. It was so right. And needed so badly. A distant wail of voices cried for delivery from captivity. How could they ignore it? God is not deaf. Wouldn't He make a way?

"Word was passed back to Greenwood headquarters: 'All go from down here. We trust the Lord for whatever it takes.'

"Then the easy smile spread over Roger's face. 'You already know the punch line,' he said. 'God did it, only He did it a little differently from the way we mortals planned. He cut the number of people and raised more money than we expected. He made it work. Amen!'"

When Roger finished his remarks and turned to General Burr to continue, according to Huffman, "It was a time of transition. Deep gratitude colored his words as he realized that the men seated before him capstoned the vision that had weighted his heart for 17 years.

"He quoted estimates of missionaries and national church leaders, that Penetration had accelerated the spread of the gospel in Ecuador by at least five years. There could be no evaluation placed on what this would mean in heavenly places."

Then Harry concluded by saying, "What we have to report should incite many others to take hold of the Great Commission." As anticipation rose to palpable level, the records were tallied and statistics revealed:

- 6,937 door-to-door visits, averaging 303 calls per day
- 108,320 pieces of gospel literature distributed
- 11,404 people attended nightly services
- 1,037 registered decisions to accept Jesus as Savior
- born-again believers filled three new churches

The men burst out with the doxology, singing "Praise God from whom all blessings flow" with the abandon and fervor of those who'd fought and won. They knew full well from Whom their strength had come. "Men For Missions International, a movement born of the Holy Spirit in the hearts of laymen, had come of age. Penetration '79 not only marked a fitting climax to its 25th year but also signaled the future."

Harry Burr added a wise and sensitive perspective. "Now it's our job to surround with prayer these we leave behind. Though we're discharged from front-line duty, we must form a vanguard on our knees. The combat has just begun."

In a long look back over the Penetration campaign, Huffman cites one standout characteristic: "great expectations from the Holy Spirit's power and presence."

"Each man," he writes, "had the assurance that the Spirit governed his life, knowledge that gave confidence and joy."

In the next issue of MFM's *ACTION* magazine, the editorial titled "A Triumph Begun" sums up the story. It appears without a byline so one can assume that Editor Eleanor Burr wrote the piece.

"Penetration '79 now belongs to heaven's annals. But the miracles of the life-changing gospel will never end. In the 30-day spiritual invasion of Ecuador's three major cities, over 1000 lives were rerouted for eternity. Husbands and wives

were reunited. Murder was thwarted. Families and relationships were restored. And the impact on the people became
clearly evident as with tears and warm embrace they reluctantly farewelled the MFM teams on December 15.

"Contrary to the original plan of massive door-to-door
literature distribution along with an invitation to nightly
evangelistic rallies, the 79ers sensed God's direction for in-
depth personal counseling in the homes. Teaming Americans
with Colombians and Ecuadorians proved to be the key, as
curiosity about the 'gringos' assured entry to almost every
home. And an unusual presence of the Holy Spirit propelled
the witness to already open hearts. 'Time and again they
dropped to their knees and begged God's forgiveness right
while we were witnessing to them,' one team member
beamed. A final tally reveals over 50% of the more than 1000
decisions for Christ consummated during the door-to-door
canvass.

"Once again God showed Men For Missions that the
cutting edge of the organization is the witnessing layman—
backed by those willing to give of themselves in intercession.
'We could feel the lift of prayer and power of conviction
which accompanied us each day,' emphasizes Harry Burr. 'In
spite of sickness, loneliness, filth, and crude living conditions, each man on the team selflessly pushed ahead. A

beautiful spirit of unity and urgency prevailed, even in the most trying circumstances. Only God could have put it all together and brought such thrilling results. We're overwhelmed and deeply grateful to all who went, sent others, gave, or prayed. The rewards in heaven will be far beyond every investment.'"

The article goes on to reflect on what the MFMers left behind after their month of intense evangelization. What can be done, what should be done after they leave?

"Let's trust Him to not only keep each of these new believers strong and faithful, but also to make them vital witnesses to the thousands around them who have yet to know God's pardon and love."

And so, in 25 years, what started out as an innovative, often inspired effort to get men off the couch and out into the world with the gospel...was doing exactly that.

And, God willing, more were on the way.

Chapter Nine

80s: Cat Skinners and Drill Sergeants

Even with Penetration '79 behind him, Harry Burr did not put his feet up on the desk and reminisce. Another plan percolated in his mind and heart. This one may not have required a folder in his much-traveled briefcase, but mentally he weighed all the angles while he persisted in seeking God's guidance.

Just weeks after returning to the U.S. from his month in Ecuador, Burr set off with an Oregon-based laymen's chorus to the British Isles. The Salem Singers, renowned in the Northwest, sing upbeat gospel music with heart, spirit, and musical polish—an ideal way to get the MFM story told among British Christians.

The Singers played vital roles both in the U.S. and overseas for MFM and OMS back as far as 1966. When OMS moved its headquarters from California to Indiana, the entire group flew to Indianapolis and sang at a gala banquet organized to introduce the mission to the area.

Then in 1976, 78 men and women financed a concert tour to the Orient, singing there in churches for OMS. Because of that trip, Myron and Eudene Snyder moved to Greenwood from the Northwest; Myron headed up the missionary car program and Eudene, with her computer skills, presided over mailing lists and maintenance records.

And in 1980, even while the Salem Singers' concerts and testimonies ministered to hundreds of lay people in Britain, part of Harry's thinking remained focused on 1983.

In '83, Harry would turn 60 and he'd decided he should relinquish MFM leadership that year.

"Quit? Whatever for?"

Questions must have bombarded MFM's executive director from all directions as co-workers, cabinet men, and OMS friends and leaders found out what he planned. Few men could be found with as much vitality, commitment, and love for God's world that he drew from daily, so why would he leave?

Harry, however, didn't want to stay too long.

Years before in the business world, Burr says, he was told, "after 60 a person seems to accomplish a little less."

Insurance gurus said one "cannot relate effectively to people either ten years your senior or ten years your junior." Harry felt "the Lord wouldn't want me to continue beyond that." Harry knew that MFM needed to connect with and mobilize younger men in order to maintain the worldwide action for which they were so well known. And true to his conviction, whether others saw it his way or not, Harry set out to "find a good man to take my place."

Circumstances did not cooperate, however—at first.

In the late 70s, OMS tapped MFM's National Director Howard Young to take charge of their national ministries department. This meant he promoted support partnerships for pastors and leaders in the countries where OMS works. It also meant that he supervised people from those countries who were studying in North America. One year later, Young took over as OMS vice president of administration. In the meantime, Jim Murray stepped into the gap as national director.

Burr worked with and coached all the men on the MFM staff, often deeply moved by the high caliber of people God called into the world that occupied him without reservation. As he studied the roster of regional directors, MFM's field reps or sales force, one stood out.

About Warren Hardig, Burr says, "I appreciated his work for years. He was loved by laymen and was always busy."

In 1981, Harry and Eleanor spent time with Warren and Velma discussing the possibility of Warren taking Harry's place.

"They seemed reluctant," Burr remembers.

Then changes began to click into place. At the January 1982 cabinet meeting in Kansas City, Jim Murray resigned as national director.

At that same meeting the men of the cabinet approved Warren Hardig to replace Murray as national director. His acceptance of this challenge put the man from Illinois under Harry's tutelage and on the leadership track one year before the Burrs' planned departure.

Warren felt "in a whirl. Honored and overwhelmed," he says, by the cabinet's unanimous decision.

"Working with him that year," Harry recalls, "I felt so comfortable about stepping aside."

Their appointment meant that the Hardigs must sell their dream home in Olney, Illinois, and move to Greenwood, Indiana. This proved difficult.

"Do we follow the Lord or stay in security?" the burly man asked more than once.

It seemed to him that missionary life could be fraught with dangers and disappointment. And yet, Hardig was attracted to the OMS emphasis on holy Christian living. He also liked the look of the missionaries. This was fortunate because in 1969, prior to his exposure to OMS, Warren says, "I really did think that missionaries were rejects. I didn't think they could cut it in America and so, for one reason or another, they went overseas."

He found another plus factor; "In MFM, I could do something that was fun and yet had value."

The Hardigs took the plunge, listed their home for sale, and moved to Greenwood so Warren could fill the national director post. Inherent in this move was Warren's apprenticeship with Harry Burr into MFM senior leadership.

In retrospect Hardig says, "MFM gave me a way to express myself. That was exciting." He certainly found plenty of personal stretching by staying in touch with 135 North American councils.

When asked for specifics, he cites "a source of solid spiritual food...I found the Word lived out. I also wanted to hear what God was doing...it gave me a passion for the lost...missions gave me an avenue to help people get saved."

The former Army drill sergeant, once expected to be tough and mean, felt comfortable with tears and vulnerability after his initial plunge into Haiti's needs. Not merely comfortable, he sought out such points of connection, eager to talk about his Savior.

And so, in July 1983, Harry Burr resigned as executive director of Men For Missions International and moved with Eleanor to Casselberry, Florida.

"I felt I shouldn't be standing over Warren," he says.

This move, however, did not represent retirement for either Burr. Eleanor continued her expert oversight of all things editorial for both MFM and OMS. This meant for her a considerable amount of commuting between Florida and Indiana. Harry became Florida regional director for the two organizations.

"God blessed us in that work," he remembers. "Archie Porter and I visited MFMers and OMS supporters who had retired in Florida."

Archie had told Harry, "If it's too far for these people to travel anymore, let's suggest that we come to them." So the two veterans of many a banquet and prayer gathering set up monthly dinners in areas of the state where MFM and OMS supporters cluster.

"Growth and involvement increased," Harry says. "We made new friends and had a good time."

At the same time, under Hardig's leadership Haiti
continued to draw MFMers, new ones and veterans. The
price to get there stood within reach of even the flattest
wallets, and the island's social and spiritual needs broke the
heart of anyone who took time enough to stop, look, and
listen. Early in 1982, all of Haiti, it seemed, celebrated an
unprecedented road-building event. Born of love and concern,
it was carried out with skill and godly grit that made onlook-
ers want to grab a pick and move a boulder or two. It began
as a determined little seedling in the heart of missionary
Hudson Hess; he tells the story in Rachael Picazo's *Let the
Rocks Cry Out*.

Hess writes about scaling the Mathieux Mountains
with Haitian Pastor Napo; they planned to visit churches
among "the barren, silent, inhospitable peaks.

"A sadness gripped me," Hudson says, "as I realized
that these mountains, now so dry and desolate, had once
proudly carried vast forests of hardwoods and pine. Could
any human being exist up there? It seemed impossible. Yet
trails curled up the slopes."

Hess and co-worker David Graffenberger accompanied
Pastor Napo to Ti Bois, a village imprisoned among those
desolate peaks. In the pitiless heat they hiked straight up, it
seemed, on a trail punctuated with boulders. "Even the path

became our enemy, radiating absorbed heat like an oven. With no shade nor place to rest, our heads throbbed and perspiration poured.

"Lord," Hudson prayed, "if You want us to reach these people for You, give us a road someday."

Since that day in 1964, Hess learned his way around those mountains, making countless trips to visit churches there. "Once I hiked 130 miles in a week," he says. And on every trip his "prayer and planning for the road continued."

Field Director Eldon Turnidge flew Hudson over the ranges in his small plane where they "saw mountain crowded upon mountain, so inaccessible that, though villagers saw lights of Haiti's capital blinking at night, many had never fought their way down to the city."

Sixty thousand farmers, among the poorest of the nation slumped at the bottom of the Western Hemisphere's economic pecking order, scratched their existence from sun-baked slopes. "They lugged their scanty produce to the city on tortuous footpaths, brushing rock walls on one side to avoid gaping ravines on the other. When sickness struck, sometimes death overtook them on the trail en route to help." Hess's heart broke as he clambered among the rocks seeking to hold out a hand of love to the people of the hardscrabble churches hidden there.

As he hiked through the region, Hudson began looking for the best way to construct a road. A local peasant's comment did nothing to encourage the missionary.

"I've watched goats on those hills since I was a child, and there's absolutely no way a road could go through."

But God had a better idea.

Surveys continued and Hess acquired help, Haitian help, with his dreams, surveys and prayers. A businessman wrote a check for enough money to buy picks and shovels, plus a bit of training in road-building techniques. MFMers in Ohio sent more tools. Other grants and aid trickled in as Hess and his helpers tried to sell the idea and elicit work time from local men who, as the dreamers knew, would profit immeasurably from the project.

Groundbreaking began in March 1972. Probably not an organized ceremony with dignitaries in dark suits wielding shiny new shovels to turn a handful of sand imported for the occasion. More likely, peasant farmers showed up and were issued picks and shovels. Julien (Hess's Haitian co-worker) may have showed them the string tied to stakes and told them to follow that string as they dug.

"It was slow at first," Hess writes. "The men lived distances away, were more interested in their gardens, and figured their time wasted anyway on something that could not be finished."

In spite of reluctance on the part of the volunteer workers and an accident that put Julien in the hospital, God did not abandon the project. Australian friends sent a Christmas offering to help build the road.

Then another setback. A boulder broke loose above the road, causing it to give way and "propelling one worker down the steep slope..."

"He's finished!" everyone cried. Hurrying to his side, Hudson writes, "The workmen found him badly lacerated—but still alive. We knew only the hand of God had kept him from death. Yet, for nearly two months, most of the men refused to work.

"'The devil doesn't want the road,' they asserted. 'He's going to kill somebody for sure if we continue.'

"But leaders from Leger, a community in the center of the mountains, heard about the road. 'If the people at Ti Bois are not interested in continuing the road,' they said, 'don't stop for them. We'll send 100 men a day to get it up here.'"

The road project inched forward, marked by rocks removed and dirt rearranged by men with a dream.

Included in the road story in *Let the Rocks Cry Out* is an article from *ACTION* magazine. The quiet, gentle Hudson

Hess, it says, boldly asked MFM for a bulldozer. In response, three men, Ohioans Bob Pipes and Clyde Bowman, plus Bob Wittig from Florida, "volunteered their mountain-dozing experience and cleared the rock with a rented bulldozer. As skilled operators, they did in a week what manual labor could not have accomplished in months.

"Bob and Clyde longed to return the following year and presented the idea of purchasing a bulldozer to the Butler Council in Ohio. Nearby councils in Bucyrus and Morrow County helped...." With that kind of backing, they found a used D8 Cat for $8000. They restored this veteran piece of heavy machinery and asked MFM founder Dwight Ferguson to dedicate it to the Lord. Within days it lumbered its way to Haiti.

"The first time Bob and Hudson took the dozer to Ti Bois (halfway to Dupin), hundreds of people appeared, to witness the arrival of the first vehicle. Hudson translated while Bob spoke to the crowd. Tears filled his eyes as he declared, 'Only in God's economy could a Cat skinner like me become a celebrity.'"

Bob Pipes had been moving mountains since he left the Marines in 1952. Backhoes, graders, bulldozers were as familiar to him as his front door. "I can almost sleep on a dozer or backhoe," he claims, so the Haiti road project drew in some of the best to push it through.

About this point, MFMers began to get serious, and plunged into the road-building project. "MFM crusaders began arriving on the scene," *ACTION* tells us. "Here was a job made to order for earthmovers. Though the highest peaks, at 5,000 feet, aren't much as mountains go, sometimes the machines teetered on the edge of nothing. More than once the snorting monsters rocked enough to frighten even guardian angels.

"More than 20 men—usually two or three at a time—made up the teams to Haiti. Clyde Bowman and Bob Pipes, both of Bellville, Ohio, returned often. With the primitive and the modern working together, a track 20 feet wide began snaking back upon itself again and again, climbing the gulch-pocked range."

Bob Pipes' memories of those days are strong and clear. When asked was he ever in danger, he says, "Constant danger!" He rode his dozer around the steep mountain shoulders, shoving rocks and dirt down the slopes, sustained by his Creator.

"A witch doctor cursed Bowman and me." They saw an evil-looking cow skull he placed in their track.

"What's that?" they asked.

"If you don't stop, you die," Satan's henchman threatened.

"Well, I serve a power stronger than the one you follow," said Pipes. He then proceeded to plow the menacing skull to the side of the road and went on with his God-given assignment. No one died.

Why did Pipes take on this job in Haiti when his own earthmoving company waited in Ohio?

"It was my ministry. Some guys are preachers but I'm not. This I can do. It's people's souls and lives. They're important!"

Then he remembers from his own experience what lies at the core of MFM. "We never took anybody to a mission field but they could do something." To illustrate, he cites the man who'd never touched a trowel but before his plane left for home he was laying block and building a church.

Would Bob Pipes do it again?

"Sure. We worked from dark to dark and it was hard but I was young. Only don't wait until you're 70."

Missionaries supervised the work teams and briefed them about not only the danger of the work but lurking tarantula spiders as well. "The men slept on a pastor's porch, ate Spam sandwiches, and took baths in a drainage ditch."

Kansas MFMers provided a road grader and World Vision bought the fuel. When the road builders reached Ti Bois, missionary Bill Glace pointed on to Leger, nine miles distant, as their next goal. "The terrain was hazardous and hard on equipment, but God sent Forrest Cammack from Oregon, who could fix broken machinery.

"As the mountains surrendered before the onslaught, missionary and national evangelistic teams plodded ahead on foot. Consequently, road builders arrived to find congregations already established by the vanguard. And better roads mean better attendance at services."

Finally came the day "in March 1982, ten years and 28 miles after the project started, Bill Glace, Bob Pipes, and a weary crew of MFMers chugged into Dupin," where, years before, MFMers from Kentucky built a church. Guys from Indiana helped to fund it, and a team of laymen "poured two weeks of love-labor into the rugged church where the Christians of Dupin worshipped.

"Now, with the road reaching into their village, a grateful crowd of Haitians cheered the completion of this highway, their outlet to the world. The MFMers, standing around the bulldozer, praised God.

"Government dignitaries, missionaries, and thousands of people held a huge celebration with a ribbon-cutting

ceremony and a feast of goat meat followed by speeches."
And most important, like priceless gems laid at the Master's
nail-scarred feet, "since then countless Haitians have come to
salvation."

Hudson Hess, who, though retired, still lives in Haiti,
says that 20 years later the road is still operable to Ti Bois.
"There are some blockages on to Leger," he says, "but I
went up in my pickup."

The best news is that five churches now flourish in Ti
Bois: Evangelical (planted by OMS), Nazarene, and Baptist.
Hess found 250 worshippers in the Evangelical congregation
when he last visited. Add to that each church's schools for the
mountain children, and the ability to travel down to the city
for medical care.

When asked if the road made any difference in the
economic situation for mountain villagers, Hess responds,
"Absolutely." And the young people are literate, better
educated then ever before versus the shy, ignorant children
who used to peep out at the strangers from behind their doors.

How did Hudson Hess feel about the road and its
effect on the region? "Of this I am sure," he wrote, "the One
who said 'I am the way, the truth, and the life,' is interested
in a way for that truth and life to penetrate the mountains of
Mathieux. It's great to have a small part in His plan."

Chapter Ten

80s: Heading Home

For Dwight Ferguson, the decade started out just fine. In 1980, the Morrow County Council in Ohio sponsored the Fergusons' participation in an MFMI trip to India. "I spent my *80th birthday* in India," Stella loved to say. Both enjoyed being again in the nation that figured so large in their early world evangelization efforts.

Soon, however, the hard-driving years began to take their toll on the health and stamina of both Fergusons. Reluctantly they decided to sell their Ohio farm and move to Indiana. Why Indiana? The Hunts, their only immediate family, now lived and worked at OMS headquarters in Greenwood, and their horde of mission-related friends turned up there most often. Which meant they could expect visits from and enjoy encounters with comrades and colleagues.

Their little white cottage on a side street became a rendez-vous, a destination for guests from around the world.

The clink of coffee cups and ripples of laughter warmed its walls as memories, news, and ideas bounced among men and women of kindred commitments. The Ferguson knees may have grown weary and slow from uncounted miles traveled but their heart passions never waned.

Dwight's lifelong habit was to nap briefly after lunch, but at the end of his snooze one day, he woke to an entirely different way of life. A stroke brought some paralysis to his left side while skewing his emotions and his reasoning to a degree.

Family and Dwight's beloved MFMers struggled to help Stella and family care for him at home but the round-the-clock task proved too difficult. Ferguson moved to a nursing facility where wife and daughter could be close and comforting. Interestingly enough, Eugene Erny, former OMS president and the one who persuaded Dwight to include the world in his work, became Ferguson's roommate. They couldn't communicate well, given their collective disabilities, but something tugged on the hearts of their visitors to realize that this pair of titans shared the same space. Erny's second son, Ed, wrote about it in *ACTION* after his father's death in 1988. He called his piece "That Day in Rome."

"It seems peculiarly fitting that for the last months of Dad's life, his roommate should be a gentleman named Ferguson—Dwight Ferguson. Dad (Eugene Erny) was 87, failing rapidly, his mind seldom clear. Dwight had just suffered a stroke that left him partially paralyzed.

"'We are old buddies,' Dwight said with a grin the day they wheeled him into Dad's room. 'We go back a long way, a *long* way.'"

Ed explained the Ferguson/Erny encounter in Rome, Georgia in 1952, ruminating on God's purpose in drawing the two into proximity again. Dwight liked to talk about that day to anyone he could corral, and Ed did not escape. He describes what he heard.

"'Listen,' Dwight told me, his eyes flashing mischievously, 'I didn't want anything to do with foreign missions. When I saw a missionary coming, I ran the other way. Missions was somebody else's job—not mine. But that day your dad cornered me in a hotel room there in Rome, and for three hours he talked missions non-stop.'"

Eugene Erny had poured the force of his own considerable devotion to mission that day into the mind and heart of the reluctant evangelist in the other chair. He nailed his prey, it seems, with the statement, "Until you let God break your heart you will never know the full ministry He has for you."

And Dwight Ferguson never wanted to miss anything.

Ed goes on to tell of the birth of Men For Missions and some of the consequences of that encounter between his father and Ferguson, the two old lions who shared the same den, an anteroom of sorts, as they awaited their invitations to come home.

In spite of doctors' predictions that Ferguson could not survive the severity of his stroke, he lingered in his limited state for another five years. Stella found living alone too stressful so she moved into a studio apartment in the same facility with Dwight and was able to visit him every day. Even though daughter Carroll and her husband, Ev Hunt, accepted a summons to spend a year working in Hong Kong, granddaughter Julie remained in Greenwood during their absence and watched over her grandparents daily.

Harry Burr posed some questions about Dwight's shrinking borders in "Eternal Treasures in Earthen Vessels" for *ACTION* magazine in 1989.

"How does one shift from traversing the front lines of the world to confinement in a wheelchair that someone else controls? What about a transition from preaching before masses in many nations to sharing a scripture verse with a nurse's aide in a rest home lounge?

"That's the adjustment required these days of Dwight Ferguson, founder of Men For Missions International.

"While a few of us gathered at the retirement home to celebrate his birthday, the ringing of a phone became paramount. In a prearranged call Dwight received a very special 'Happy Birthday' from Carroll Hunt, his missionary daughter then serving in Hong Kong. His smile made evident the deep meaning of that moment. But after the call came the realization that probably neither he nor his voice will cross the ocean again.

"It was then I asked if he and Stella could still agree with the psalmist in 'Bless the Lord...and all that is within me bless His holy name.'

"'Absolutely,' they quickly chorused."

Burr, who served as surrogate son and a most satisfying disciple to Ferguson, noted that to visit Dwight and Stella with their comfort in mind, more likely meant the reverse. "You leave under sunnier, bluer skies—with new hope perched in your horizon.

"The years have eroded their physical frames, but the inner strength shows no sign of aging or decline.

"With faltering speech but unimpaired thought, Dwight still ably excavates treasures from God's Word—and with characteristic chuckle eagerly shares his discovery."

Ferguson, until his death, remained confident that if only he could be in the same place with people who needed "the message," he would still be of service in building the Kingdom. Before their departure he often urged Carroll, his daughter, to make arrangements to take him along to Hong Kong and put him in a room to which people would come, where he could minister to them from his "cart," his name for his wheelchair.

Burr continues with what Ferguson had to say regarding his situation: "'Of course we get lonely and the devil attacks on every front,' Dwight confesses. 'But this is our place of service now.' Then, opening his Bible to II Corinthians 4:7-11 he shares his exhilaration regarding the real estate God's preparing for their homecoming.

"'Nothing can keep that from happening. It's sure because Christ promised it,' he says through joy-filled tears."

After his family returned from Hong Kong, Dwight Ferguson decided his time to go home had come. With a remarkably sweet smile and clear, knowing blue eyes, he refused medicine and food...and within hours he was gone.

"'Tell them to tell the Story; tell them to plant the seed.' Those were Dwight's last words as I left an interview session with the beloved founder of Men For Missions

International." So begins Ron Mertens' tribute in *ACTION*, which he called "An Exceptional Servant of God."

"The message Dwight imparted with that statement will burn in my heart unendingly.

"Forever the evangelist, Dwight sent similar words into the deepest recesses of hearts the world over. Born with acutely penetrating eyes, Dwight had an unswerving, even demanding way of enlisting men into God's service."

Mertens had watched his subject carefully. He pinpointed Ferguson's methods and passions accurately, recapping the effect of them on his world.

"Dwight was also a soul-saver. Setting a radical example among fashionable pastors and evangelists, Dwight took the story of Jesus to those who had never seen a collection plate. He could do so because he's accepted Christ's command, 'Be holy because I am holy....'

"Guided by the Holy Spirit, Dwight realized that only laymen had sufficient ranks to spread the gospel into every corner of earth. Word by word, prayer by prayer, he challenged laymen for over 30 years."

Mertens concludes by thanking God "for giving us Dwight, for through him we were taught how common men can invest their lives in eternal work. We've caught Dwight's vision of Mark 3:14, where a compassionate Jesus appointed 12 laymen and sent them out to spread the Word.

"'Now,' asserted Dwight, 'because Men For Missions is of God's will, it's not 12 men, it's thousands; instead of donkeys, it's jet planes; instead of Galilee, it's the world.'"

Yes, the man who created an uproar by saying, "I never got thrilled about going to a knitting party with my grandmother," left in his wake thousands of men who'd decided *not* to leave it to the "little woman" to take care of the church's mission to the world. Men who'd jumped in with both feet and did something about human poverty, spirit as well as body.

But what did Dwight Ferguson really mean by this remark that may have sounded like a stereotypical male putdown of women's activities? What is Men For Missions' organizational attitude toward women beneath the resounding maleness of their rhetoric?

Enloe Wallar's widow, Irene, offers her seasoned view in an article she wrote for "The Feminine Touch," a feature in *ACTION* in 1989. In this article she used the "knitting party" quote as her lead. "These words," she said, "were the call that brought Men For Missions into existence."

Did Irene feel fenced out when Enloe "followed Dwight into that room?" Apparently not.

"It not only changed his life, but mine as well," she wrote. "As our participation in this new movement increased, the Holy Spirit convinced me that every Christian is to accept the Master's invitation to 'go and make disciples of all nations.' As a result, MFM became a very special part of my inner being. As a family we dedicated ourselves to do, go, and give as divinely directed."

Irene celebrated her husband's 28-year-long faithfulness to MFM. She also cites the service of the four Wallar daughters in Haiti, Ecuador, and Hong Kong, plus in their home churches. "The greatest heritage one can bestow upon children," she claims, "is love for the gospel message and the doing, going, and giving embraced by MFM."

The Wallar home on its hill in Mt. Carmel, Illinois, stood with doors open to traveling missionaries. Bible studies and intercessory prayer meetings taught many of their neighbors about opportunities to share their faith abroad. "All this, plus supporting MFM through Lifeliners and numerous projects, reminds me that as a feminine contributor I have unique responsibilities. But I love these responsibilities because I accept Christ's words: 'For unto whomsoever much is given, of him shall much be required.'

"God has abundantly blessed me over the years, and much of that blessing has come about through MFM."

Irene's positive take on a woman's welcome into MFM raises another question: How does an avowedly male movement manage to make women welcome participants in its goals?

A couple of quotes from the past shed some light.

"One of the things that made me get under the load of Men For Missions in the early days was our experience in India. I was appalled at seeing women doing man-sized jobs." So spoke missionary and first Executive Director Dale McClain from retirement. He didn't mean that women weren't qualified or authorized to do whatever came to hand. He groaned over the lack of men's interest, involvement, participation. Their failure to take on winning the world for Christ.

Looking back over almost 50 years of MFM involvement, Archie Porter speaks on the matter from a wise and pragmatic point of view: "Our council attendance was poor as a men-only event. The fellows didn't come regularly. Our wives sat at home and felt excluded. In 1976 I shifted the meetings to our home and invited the wives. Attendance began to pick up and our average jumped to 50."

These council meetings over an approximately 30-year span have provided more than $280,000 for missionary support and projects. One wonders if the lavish buffets Mary

Lou serves at each session has anything to do with such generosity. And she pays for every morsel from her own funds, counting this as her own personal ministry.

In early 1989, *ACTION* editor Ron Mertens wrote a brief editorial urging more writers to contribute to "For Women Only."

"Attention wives, daughters, mothers, sisters: We hope you have noticed our special tribute to you in each issue of *ACTION*. It takes shape in the article entitled, 'The Feminine Touch,' and is our way of recognizing your contribution to Christ through Men For Missions. Your influence, time and gifts are of boundless value to both the man and his mission, and we affirm your enormous boost with deeply felt sincerity."

Mertens explains the feature and urges his feminine readers to contribute their points of view regarding MFM and its role in world evangelization. He offers editorial aid, if needed, and says that the "important thing is that it convey a message to benefit others spiritually."

Lois Schultz's husband, John, was president of Men For Missions in the late 80s. She wrote from experience when she said, "I really believe that as a direct result of John's involvement with MFM, we have a more loving husband and father in our home. It has made him a tremendous example and vibrant spiritual leader, yet a man with a broken heart for the lost world. Because he is completely dedicated to doing, going, and giving, wonderful results are apparent in our family. Our oldest son is becoming more and more involved in the local church. Our other son will go on his fourth crusade this summer, having completed his second year in Bible college as a missions major.

"It is exciting to see what God does when we promise to do, go, and give. Great is His faithfulness."

Warren Hardig sums it up: "Men For Missions is not for the exclusion of ladies but for the inclusion of men."

And the women whose menfolk dive into the MFM mainstream seem mighty pleased with their own piece of the action.

Chapter Eleven

90s: Wider, Longer, Higher, Deeper

Warren Hardig's 1991 trip opened new vistas for him and for Men For Missions International.

"I went with an OMS survey team to Hungary along with Bill Anderson from Scotland and missionary David Cosby," Hardig says. "I sensed God's special presence. It was like there was another person with us."

OMS was weighing the possibility of opening mission work in that country and Warren's inclusion on the team created far-reaching effects for him and for MFMI. Talks with local Christians and an opportunity to tell the Hungarian vice-president about his spiritual pilgrimage merged with other encounters and events to open even wider Hardig's window on his world.

"It was a great trip for me," he says. By this he means that he learned to care deeply about Eastern Europeans, and the caring burst into flame on his first trip into post-cold-war Russia. The ministry that followed, which resembled something an MFMI team was doing in the U.S. and South America, stretched the imagination and resources of those who got involved.

After investigating Russian needs and opportunities where newly-free people struggle to find their footing, Hardig initiated a new kind of MFMI overseas "ministry team." He and several other people—including Jim Acheson, Peter and Judy Wozniuk, John McLaughlin, Maury Graham, and Velma Hardig—began offering business seminars, not to presume superiority or to dominate by their teaching, but rather to dialog with interested men and women. They promoted interchange, conversations about business ethics, or the ins and outs of decision-making and record-keeping—anything of interest to those who came to talk and learn. Always, Warren and his teammates spoke of God's laws and His love, usually by means of their personal stories of coming to faith and how that faith affects the way they do business.

Three times each year an MFMI team journeyed to one of the Russian cities, or to Estonia or Kazakhstan. Were they welcome? Relevant? Did erstwhile Communists tolerate talk of God?

"In Ivanova, Russia," Hardig remembers, "a business school instructor spoke English and so questioned us face to face. 'Who are you?' he demanded to know."

Warren told how he, a businessman eager to make money, had turned his life over to God, thereby learning how to work according to His guidelines. The teacher's reaction to his story? Simple, direct, and revealing his strong interest. "Come back," he said.

Hardig and his teams worked from a careful plan. After receiving an invitation to a specific place, they created three-day sessions. In those sessions, the MFMers, through a Russian interpreter, discussed ways to treat business competitors or how to write business plans. They also delved into a wide spectrum of ethical issues. The MFMers strove to learn about those with whom they talked, to discover their level of knowledge and expertise. And what they learned often surprised them, as when they were discussing money management. A hand went up and the interpreter passed on the question: "What are accounts receivable?"

In reflecting on recurring themes, Warren remembers that the matter of trust loomed large. "They had no trust in others," he says, "and that issue was always a hard thing."

Plenty of prayer went before every session and afterwards the team often huddled far into the night. Like a football team on the offensive, they altered and amplified their curriculum plans as they allowed for what they had learned about the people with whom they were talking. Nothing was set in stone; flexibility reigned. They seized every opportunity available to speak of the importance of personally relating to the Lord. As in one session when Warren claimed, "I found something more meaningful than making money."

"What was that?" a skeptical listener shot the question back at him. Hardig proceeded to tell about his encounter with God, of course, and asserted that Jesus Christ is the only foundation available on which to build trust, that missing commodity in the Russian business community.

Over a period of five years, some 250 people made up the 11 ministry teams that participated in MFMI's unique evangelism effort in Russia and other Eastern European countries.

"They got into us, into our hearts," Warren Hardig says. "We couldn't get rid of them!"

The business seminars drew from an earlier effort Harry Burr—who else—fielded across the U.S. and into Colombia. Ron Mertens wrote about it in *ACTION* in 1995 under the title, "God Owns My Business." He described a dinner gathering in Indiana where Stanley Tam, perhaps

MFMI's pilot model, told simply and calmly how God had led him to put Him first. How obedience caused his business to flourish and how that flourishing provides $2.6 million dollars annually for world evangelism through OMS.

"An elated and grateful MFMI staff soon recognized God's nudge toward a totally new outreach. Harry Burr, Warren Hardig, and Bill Spate met to pray and seek His guidance. Encouraged by others, Harry went to Stanley's office for a marathon discussion on the possibilities of challenging business owners to follow Tam's example.

"On February 10, 1993, the new program called 'God Owns My Business' was born of God at the initial dinner in Clearwater, Florida.

"A quick review paints an astounding picture. In the first 18 months, 202 people either accepted Christ as Savior or recommitted their lives to Him. In addition, 148 men and women dedicated their businesses to God.

"The program format begins with a Friday evening dinner geared to reaching unsaved friends and family members. The next day, Harry and Stanley team up with Lou Mayer and other qualified experts for a five-hour (including lunch) seminar."

Burr and Tam taught during those hours that the concept means "the complete integration of all Christian principles into every aspect of business," truths that Warren Hardig and his teams would soon share in Eastern Europe. "There can be no separation of Christian values," Mertens continued, "ethics, and practices between one's private and business life. They are totally blended together with Christ at the head."

While the majority of men who visited mission work with MFMI still went to nations close to North America, some, as had been the case through the years, launched out to India, China, Japan, and Russia. In 1995, men of a work team packed their tools, boarded a trans-Pacific flight, and landed in Hong Kong. In that over-crowded bit of China they repaired missionary flats for OMS International.

In fact, between 1989 and 1999, 54 men and women on four work teams spent time in Hong Kong. What for? Missionary Cindy Aufrance writes about the difference these people made: "In terms that can be quantified, they saved us thousands of dollars in labor costs for maintenance and the upkeep of our flats. In less measurable terms, they brought encouragement to us with their joyful attitude of serving, even in the heat, humidity, language challenges, and materials they had never seen before. It is such a joy to work with people who invest themselves in doing an excellent and thorough job, no matter how big or small the task.

"And some of the teams contacted local believers in English classes, giving their testimonies, etc. They impacted lives. They impressed local Chinese that Western Christians would pay their own expenses to come here and do a job that doesn't carry a lot of respect, in local estimation. In other words, these believers *paid* to serve rather than serving in order to get paid. By serving us in this way, they free us to continue serving the people of Hong Kong, as God called us to do.

"And I know we as a field benefit by their prayers and the broader world view they acquired through their time here in Hong Kong. Each of these people occupies a special place in my heart for contributing to our ministry in Hong Kong."

Similar teams with like purpose went to Ecuador, where along with the ever-needed building upkeep they also installed radio equipment in Carboncillo, OMS International's mountain outpost.

In Spain, maintenance and improvements are a perpetual need and MFMI provides expertise and countless work hours to see that this need is met.

In Russia, Maury Graham, a retired banker from Montana, hosted three work teams in one year, men and women who transformed a business building into a seminary where future Christian leaders receive their training for ministry.

And how did Graham make the shift from Montana to Moscow? What was MFMI's influence on his life?

"Pretty profound, actually," he says. Ever since the 1960s when Maury Graham became a Christian believer, missionaries were a part of his life as they came and went through his church. OMS and MFM came up on his screen and introduced a shift in all his purposes, so much so that he took his teenage children to Haiti in 1973.

"Missions became real to me when I got to a field," Graham says.

After the death of his wife, Heidi, he knew he didn't want to stay home. "Now what, Lord?" he prayed.

In response to Graham's query of God, missionary friend Dave Graffenberger, who'd transferred from Haiti to mission work in Russia, invited Maury to Moscow. At the end of the visit, Dave asked the former banker to assume responsibility for mission finances in Russia. That was 1996; the man from Montana has not looked back since.

Someone else does the treasurer's job in Russia for OMS International now but Graham still doesn't sit at home. Nor does he have time to play much golf with his retired friends in Arizona. OMS International fields evangelism teams all over the world and Maury says, "Now I spend most of my time in Kazakhstan and Hungary," where he shepherds the men of the teams in those countries.

But that's not all the wiry, active Montanan puts his hand to. "I sometimes do special assignments for Warren," he admits. Which means he could turn up in China or Spain or Scotland on behalf of MFMI.

"I just want to find out what the Lord has in mind for me. He sustains me."

That much is clear as Graham hops on and off planes like some people go to the post office or gas station, untroubled by jet lag or culture shock. For this he thanks his Lord.

"He put into my heart a desire to serve Him, to seek His will," Maury acknowledges. "I'm glad I am able to do this." The globetrotting retiree also claims, "Age doesn't make the difference, willingness does."

And closer yet to home, other men with hearts also willing to work and time to take action, help out with building and repair at the OMSI/MFMI hub in Greenwood, Indiana. There they've painted walls, rearranged partitions, improved utilities, poured new cement, renewed landscaping. This, and so much more, reflects the action of men who stand always available to the Lord's call to service.

A second 1997 issue of *ACTION,* runs a column defining Men For Missions International. It says in part, "MFMers help missionaries by releasing their personal skills and abilities in a variety of practical, direct ways. Included are work teams, teams that help with local evangelism, teams that go to pray and distribute tracts (*Intercessors*) and others who are prepared to teach. Often, teams may be involved in one or more of these ministries.

"MFMI has no dues nor formal trappings. We exist to serve Christ by assisting OMS International. Our mandate is compassion, pure and simple. Our priority is establishing the lordship of Jesus Christ in each man's life, and our goal is to provide opportunities for personal obedience to the Great Commission."

Loren Minnix, appointed cabinet president in 1995, told how he felt about MFMI and its purposes:

"I love Men For Missions because it's a group of men who love the Lord. You come to take action, not just talk about it. You come because you care for the lost and dying. You're electricians who handle the power of God; farmers who plant the seed of the Word; bankers who know about riches in Christ; insurance men who sell eternal plans; plumbers who pipe living water to thirsty souls; carpenters who build sanctuary and shelter; and godly men who give their all to the cause of Christ. I want you to know that I'm proud to be among you."

Calculations at the time reveal that MFMI saved OMSI $39,000 in trucking and shipping costs; $93,000 in the U.S. and $145,000 overseas with volunteer labor; $50,000 in equipment and material supplied without cost to the mission.

No one in MFMI seems to forget, however, that all their effort is about people who need to know the Creator personally. In "Wow, What a Ride," *ACTION* 1997, Archie Porter, one of the first men to catch the vision, writes, "Can you believe it? I went on my first Men For Missions trip 40 years ago. Not only on my first trip with MFMI, but also on the first trip MFMI ever made.

"I'll never forget the observation of our Missionary Aviation Fellowship pilot as we swooped low over a village in Ecuador's jungle. 'Do you see those villagers looking up at us?' he asked.

"'Sure do,' I responded.

"'Archie,' he replied, 'they have never heard the name of Jesus.'

"That remark has stayed with me all these years. Suddenly realizing there were people in the world who had never heard the gospel, I was truly staggered. That revelation resulted in a lifetime of mission involvement.

"I've since participated in 15 exciting missions trips with Men For Missions. Originally tied to a local vision, my wife Mary Lou and I would probably never have gone outside the U.S. if it had not been for MFMI. But we did, and what a ride it's been.

"First, MFMI altered the focus of our prayers from a local perspective to needs of the world. It changed the way we gave our resources and prompted us to give both money and time to mission work.

"Our travel also changed. Instead of going to U.S. resorts on our vacations, we went to mission fields. I often think of how MFMers have benefited the missionaries by building churches, clinics, and missionary homes, and doing loads of maintenance work. Our business life was affected as well. Before we sold our business, we supplied window coverings for the OMS headquarters and all the OMS fields free of charge.

"Finally, our home life changed. We bought a roomy house to allow missionaries to stop over while leaving or arriving in the U.S. Then in 1976 I relocated our MFMI council meeting to our home and invited the wives. Boy, did that idea catch on! Friends brought friends, and the attendance shot up dramatically. Once we had 93 people. This new arrangement was also a blessing to Mary Lou, since she loves hospitality and prepares a scrumptious table.

"Another blessing stemming from our involvement with MFMI was invitations to speak at MFMI dinners and in churches of MFMers across America. Sharing how God worked in our lives gave me a good opportunity to challenge others. I also felt privileged to serve on the MFMI cabinet.

"We can never thank the Lord enough for leading us to MFMI, because we've been deeply rewarded. If you want to be involved in missions, try MFMI—it's the right ticket!"

Not a bad endorsement from one of Dwight Ferguson's earliest targets.

Another event in 1997 was Stella Ferguson's promotion to heaven on May 4. She joined Dwight there, along with her son, Marvin, and son-in-law Everett Hunt. Her tribute in *ACTION* concludes with, "Because Dwight's heart for itinerant evangelism kept him on the move, Stella was mother and father for weeks at a time to their two children, Marvin and Carroll. When Dwight and Stella joined OMS International, they began traveling from country to country in the interest of worldwide missions. In this work they both enjoyed many happy and fruitful years of ministry.

"Stella was a blessing and positive example to all who knew her. OMS and MFMI will miss this remarkable woman."

As the world focused on the impending onset of a new millennium, in 1999 the Holy Spirit began whispering to one man the Lord's plans for MFMI's newest evangelism venture. A plan that would stretch and challenge MFMI and OMS International beyond their widest experience heretofore—one that would confront Satan in his own territory and could mean life or death to a whole nation.

Chapter Twelve

The 21st Century: Operation Saturation

Wayne King frowned in perplexity. Trailer trash? He knew full well where his grandsons picked up the phrase, one common enough in the U.S. nowadays. The boys enjoyed every luxury and privilege that teenagers hanker for; "do without" didn't appear in their vocabulary. So, to them, those who ride around in rusty, dusty, old cars seem to come from another planet.

King, trained in finance, had worked for OMS International in stewardship. He knew about MFMI's ministry teams and decided that a trip to Haiti would show his grandsons more of their world than they'd ever encountered. The ideal solution, he believed. He bundled the boys onto a plane along with a group of Canadian MFMers on their way to build a church in Port au Prince. His plan seemed to work.

"After we got there," King grins, "I didn't see them all day!"

Caleb and Joshua joined the Canadians and grabbed hold of a corner of the church building job and didn't let go until it was finished. They learned about helping to solve a problem rather than ridicule those struggling with it.

"It was an excellent week," Wayne says. "Those boys saw what men of faith could be...and Caleb even gave his clothes to a Haitian boy."

Introducing his grandsons to God's waiting world—in addition to learning that most Haitians can neither read nor afford radios—served as a launch pad that synchronized Wayne King's mind and heart with what the Creator was about to use him to lay on MFMI's sturdy shoulders. Something beyond the wildest efforts they'd ever tackled.

Anxious to avoid claiming any scrap of credit, when King faces questions about his role in the conception of Operation Saturation, he emphasizes, "Not my idea. Not Wayne King's inspiration. I cannot usurp God's glory."

What is Operation Saturation? What is the concept that King credits to God alone?

The strategy is spelled out in *interACTION*, MFMI's newsletter dedicated to the project. "Operation Saturation," it says, "is a five-year, seven-phase plan to reach Haiti for Christ through small, fix-tuned, solar-powered radios."

The seven phases read as follows:

1. Construct and equip a new broadcast center.
2. Build digital satellite uplink and five downlink sites to reach all of Haiti.
3. Saturate Haiti with thousands of small fix-tuned, solar powered radios.
4. Launch an evangelistic radio campaign to reach Haiti through the fix-tuned radios.
5. Minister to new believers, new and existing churches, while training Haitian laypeople to reach their own countrymen.
6. Underwrite much of the ongoing operational expense.
7. Saturate with warfare prayer the entire project.

Operation Saturation came out of King's thoughts on radio distribution in Haiti...on marketing radio there...about evangelism, 4VEH studio expansion needs...future endowment....

"But these ideas are certainly not part of OMSI methodology," came to his mind as a recurring deterrent. Driving along the interstate highway, King grappled with the breech between this vision and reality as he saw it.

"God, I will even put up my own retirement money to see this done—but if it's not Your plan, take it away!"

The Lord's quieting hand came over King's heart and mind. His peace moved in. Back in Indiana, Wayne bounced his ideas off Gene Bertolet, friend, veteran OMSI/MFMI staffer, and devoted Bible student.

"That would be a good project," Gene acknowledged.

"Yeah, but it's not in the OMS pattern," King spoke of the blockade he feared would prevent the idea from seeing fruition.

In spite of this fear, King talked with Warren Hardig about the ideas rotating in his mind. Hardig caught the spark and asked King to present OpSat to the MFMI Cabinet. The cabinet calmly voted to accept the five-year, $4.5 million project. No dissension.

Next, along with headquarters administrators, OMS International leaders from overseas heard Wayne's presentation. They gave their okay, as did the OMS International trustees. So far, so good.

Perhaps the most radical departure from the norm, however, lurked in the fact that much of the responsibility for the Haitian evangelism scheme lay on the narrow shoulders of a square-headed yellow cartoon character called Sonny Solar. Cartoons usually mean kids. Nothing childlike appears in the five-part strategy. That's all serious stuff about using radio to lead Haitians to faith in Jesus Christ.

What's with the cartoons?

"When I was a kid," Wayne King remembers, "missions was my connection with the world. Kids learn by listening and observing. We need the children to care as they grow up."

The marketing strategist in King looks at the possibilities. "Wherever kids go, you get all these parents and grandparents, too. If you want parents' attention, go to the kids."

Gene Bertolet, artist, and Wayne King, finance expert and grandfather, brainstormed how to make OpSat come alive to children and adults; Sonny Solar emerged from doodles and conversation in a Burger King restaurant. The yellow cartoon guy with the big square head represents the pre-tuned, solar-powered radios being distributed by the thousands in Haiti for one purpose alone—to introduce women and men and children to the Lord Jesus Christ.

Sonny Solar "has made a difference with kids," claims King. He's right. Consider: Sonny Solar in his yellow van showed up at a vacation Bible school at the United Methodist Church in Niceville, Florida.

Sonny appeared there each day, cheering on a contest between girls and boys as to who could raise the most money to buy radios for Haiti. And their pastor promised that if the total reached $5,000, he'd get his hair dyed.

On Friday night 500 kids plus a multitude of parents whooped and screamed their joy when they heard the total--$6100!

And they're still talking in Niceville about the Methodist preacher's green hair.

King describes OMS's stalwart constituency as "aging, not wealthy, with strong love for missions, and giving sacrificially" to send the Good News around the world.

"OpSat has crossed over into new territory. It goes beyond our norm to attract others," he claims.

For starters, the website, *www.sonnysolar.com*, offered interested kids special coloring books. The entire printing of 125,000 disappeared within weeks. People from India, Mexico, Russia and Ecuador have sent money to buy radios for Haiti.

As he ponders what is happening with his precedent-shattering campaign, King observes, "Tradition is an extremely valuable thing to hold onto so long as it doesn't stymie the future—tradition applied rather than tradition worshipped." The OpSat concept allows the trying of new things.

Meanwhile, Sonny Solar shows up in his yellow van at every church and school that invites him. People of all ages are getting in on the fun of learning and sharing in the task of telling Haitians about the Savior. Because of this, radios pour into the island, towers go up, broadcasts invade Satan's fortresses...and many pray.

Wayne King knows that time is short. The Haitian government talked for several years about wanting to re-dedicate Haiti to Satan, something the slaves did over 200 years ago at the onset of their revolution against French plantation owners. Operation Saturation began, in part, as a means to overwhelm the island with the power of the presence of God, thereby defeating Satan and breaking his hold on the people in that place. The date for the dedication, 1 January 2004, came and went with no dedication ceremony in sight. All the forms of evangelism set in motion by OpSat are still drawing Haitians to Jesus Christ. The year 2004 rolls on, soaked in the prayers of people around the world. By 2005 MFMI and OMS expect to see radio expansion up and running, and the evangelism thrust moving on under its own power.

What then?

"Oh, Sonny Solar has lots of friends, other critters and characters," Wayne grins. So it appears that the man with a head for marketing and a heart for God's world has more than one weapon in his arsenal, resources on call when the Lord decides to use them. One wonders what comes next.

Meanwhile, Wayne King ponders a question: What can MFMI do for the future?

"We can learn to pray," he fires back. "When men pray, they teach their sons to pray."

*****

Gene Bertolet was *not* pleased when Warren Hardig asked him to do the cabinet devotionals in Waco, Texas. Not pleased at all. He walked into Velma Hardig's office with a scowl on his face and dropped into a chair in front of her desk.

"Warren just ruined my whole Christmas," he announced without preamble.

"What did he do?" Velma asked.

"I'm so upset! He asked me to do cabinet devotions!"

Velma, wise enough to avoid futile arguments, merely said, "I agree with his choice."

Bertolet, a Bible student who comes up with scriptural insights that are anything but run-of-the-mill, heartily dislikes being drawn into public ministry. Quiet and introverted, at work he prefers the solitude of an out-of-traffic-patterns office with only the drawing board and Bible for company. The trouble is, MFMers, OMSers, and a large segment of the community of Greenwood are discovering Bertolet's insightful, no-nonsense style of communicating biblical truth. Which is why Hardig wanted the cabinet to feast on that truth as the Lord speaks it to Gene Bertolet.

In Waco after his "ruined" Christmas, the reluctant speaker laid out challenges for the men in his time with the cabinet. Operation Saturation burned on his mind because for months he'd prayed over the project and scoured Scripture for insight on God's methods of doing battle with Satan. An MFM brochure called "Circles of 8 for Haiti" tells what he came up with without naming Gene Bertolet:

"The MFMI Cabinet met for three days in January 2000, in Waco, Texas. On the final morning, an MFMI staffer who led the daily devotions, focused our attention on the need for strategic and tactical prayer. Six months earlier the Cabinet had accepted the challenge to saturate the country of Haiti with the gospel through fix-tuned radios. Now it was time to get serious about launching a strategic attack through prayer. He presented the concept of prayer warfare, using military terms to describe what we had to do. Explaining in detail, from personal experience, the concepts of prayer mapping, and praying for a whole country and its people, he reminded us that Charles Cowman, founder of OMS, prayed for China using a giant map of the country.

"The leader then proposed the following plan. There are nine administrative districts in Haiti. So, we need nine men, a man for each district to be the key person for strategic intercession. Then we need nine circles of eight prayer warriors each, that's a circle of eight for each district. Four in each circle will focus on Haiti, the other four will hold up in prayer those praying for Haiti (the Moses, Aaron, and Hur concept from Exodus 17). When intercessors go on the attack, we can expect counter attacks. So, while four pray for Haiti, four others will be praying for their protection, families, and work, while praying also for their area of Haiti.

"The leader paused and abruptly threw out a challenge. 'We need nine volunteers for this task. Count the cost. Now with heads up and eyes wide open, if you feel God wants you to be one of the nine, stand.'

"Within seconds, nine men were standing. Not eight, not ten, but nine. No one else moved. The leader, obviously as moved as the rest of us, counted again and confirmed it.

'We have our nine!'

"The rest of us gathered around the nine, laid hands on them, and prayed. Some were also agreeing to be one of their circles of eight. Then we sang, 'No turning back!'"

The brochure writer explains the concept of praying for Operation Saturation and the spiritual battle involved.

"This is spiritual warfare and none dare enter this battle lightly, or alone. Some, like Joshua, will be called upon to engage the enemy on Haitian soil. Others, like Moses will sense a call to position themselves in direct intercession for Haiti and those in the spiritual battle. Still others, like Aaron and Hur, will be needed to focus intercession on those zeroed in on the battle.

"Nine MFMers have volunteered to lead the prayer charge into their assigned district of Haiti. Each of them is like a Moses, a primary intercessor FOR THE WARFARE IN THEIR DISTRICT. Each needs three more Moses-types to join him in PRIMARY intercession in order to surround the objective with a team of four.

"Between the four PRIMARY INTERCESSORS are four SUPPORT INTERCESSORS. These are the Aarons and Hurs. They are "lifting the hands" and focusing their intercession on the four PRIMARY INTERCESSORS on behalf of their devotional life, spiritual welfare, health, families, businesses, etc."

The brochure goes on to recruit intercessors "on behalf of Haiti's seven million souls in Satan's grip." It urges readers to form and register prayer groups, "circles of eight."

From the beginning, when Bertolet accepted the appointment to head MFMI's prayer offensive, he knew he had hold of something serious. "More than ceremonial blessing," he calls it. "It's all-out war, warfare to break spiritual bondage." Quoting again from the "Circles of 8" brochure, one reads about Haiti's predicament.

"In 1791 the slave population of Haiti made a solemn pact with Satan. In exchange for victory over Napoleon's army—Haiti was a French colony at the time—they would grant Satan dominion over the nation for 200 years."

Voodoo and Satan worship are a way of life in Haiti, perhaps the poorest nation in the Western Hemisphere. This evil gripping the minds and hearts of people there sends them into frenzied worship rituals accompanied by wild drumbeats and controlled by demons. Witch doctors siphon off what little money most devotees have with promises of healing and solutions to pressing problems.

Another ominous effort by Haiti's government under-scores the seriousness of the problem. Retired Haiti mission-ary Valeene Hayes describes it in *interACTION*, Summer 2003.

"As 2004 approaches, the president of Haiti has ordered 25,000 voodoo drums to be placed in schools as part of the curriculum to reacquaint children with the 'traditions' of Haiti. The purpose of the drums in traditional voodoo rituals is to summon the spirits and then stimulate and guide the participants in worship. Half of Haiti's population is under 15 years of age."

Fortunately this is not the only effort to capture the minds and hearts of Haiti's school children. Operation Saturation is providing a 16-page Creole language prayer guide for them. "Included in the simple guide to learning how to pray," Valeene continues, "is a prayer to invite Jesus into one's heart. Already many children have prayed to accept Him as Savior. The initial printing order (funded in part by a foundation and gifts from Bible Literature International) was for 25,000. While printing was in process MFMI decided that four prayer guides should symbolically surround each voodoo drum. Within hours, God moved in the hearts of donors and...the printing order was increased to 100,000! Pray that the children of Haiti will hear the call of Jesus rather than the voice of 'traditional' voodoo drums."

The nine men who stood in commitment to pray that January day in Waco lead prayer teams into their respective districts where they walk among the villages, meet with resident Christians leaders and share their faith whenever appropriate. Their most important action, however, is the time they spend praying for the territory, behavior even some Christian Haitians did not understand.

Pastors looked at the men of Sector One's prayer team with skeptical eyes. They got right to what they considered the point of the encounter.

"Did you bring money?"

The team leader used words from the Bible. "Silver and gold have we none...but we are praying for you."

"Do you know anything about the evil involved here?" The beleaguered pastors still stood aloof, full of doubts about the visiting foreigners.

Howard Young, businessman and former missionary to France, began reciting the names of the villages in the sector, one by one in perfect French.

"We've been praying for your towns," he said.

The atmosphere warmed considerably at this revelation of the men's knowledge of their territory. The Haitians began to relax. "Things are changing," they admitted, "...and we didn't know why. Now we know."

The Haitian pastors and the MFMI prayer team then gathered around a map of the nation spread on the floor. From that circle arose prayers for Haiti from hearts united toward one goal, that Haiti be wrested from the hands of Satan and given the chance to meet the Savior.

Chapter Thirteen

The 21ˢᵗ Century: Operation Saturation II

Because of prayer, because of vision, skilled laymen with more than enough to do have assumed heavy responsibility for the mechanics of making Operation Saturation happen.

John McLaughlin leads the team. A veteran of a month in Ecuador with Penetration '79 and a lengthy history of caring about the rest of the world, John heads a business that fabricates garbage truck bodies which he markets in the U.S. and China. "A medium-sized company," he calls it, with 150 employees. Piled on top of this, he pilots OpSat as project director. McLaughlin calls this "a spiritual adventure" which he will never forget.

"It was the start of big things and of seeing God work in miraculous ways almost daily," is how John characterizes his volunteer post. "It so far has been the greatest experience of my life. I have seen God move mountains and defeat the enemy in battle after battle. My life will never be the same."

McLaughlin outlines his project manager job description: "It's the boss...where the buck stops. I put together a team and plan where to go (with the project) and with whom."

Why get into something this outsized and demanding?

Simple.

"I volunteered for leadership because it was needed," he says. "I think of Operation Saturation as an army of volunteers. To complete the ranks, God has called men and women and their families from all of North America and beyond. This army has no special training but is made up of believers who offered to give their time, talents, skills, money, and most important, their prayers. They have one thing in common. They are dedicated to defeat the enemy."

In July 2001, McLaughlin, in his leadership capacity, sent a memo to the OpSat steering committee:

"Please review the Statement of Work for Operation Saturation. This is our playbook or road map to help us get to our destination and win the game. We are a team. Much has been accomplished, but much has not been. Please give it some soul-searching. The ques-

tions: Have I done all that I committed myself to do? What do I need to do to fulfill my
promise to God and OpSat? This is the greatest opportunity some of us will ever have to
serve God and make a difference in the
world. Let's not tire when the race isn't even
half over. Let's not point fingers but take a
deep breath and run harder than ever. I can
see the victory line. Can you? 'We will reap
a harvest if we do not give up.'" (Galatians
6:9)

Warren Hardig asked McLaughlin to take the project
director job, presuming, he admits, on their long, strong
friendship. "I needed someone to give quality time to this
because OpSat is 100 times bigger than anything Men For
Missions International has ever done before."

Hardig knew John could coordinate the men responsible for construction, funding, prayer and evangelism—all
crucial components of the Haiti project. He felt confident in
John's ability to make sure the other leaders stayed on budget
and schedule, knowing he would give daily attention when
necessary.

McLaughlin grasps the scope of the challenge. "The
battle plan for Operation Saturation," he says, "was so big

and virtually impossible that the army assembled in blind faith and waited upon God for the marching orders. The first phase of the battle plan to free Haiti from the enemy called for the construction of a two-story modern broadcast center for Radio 4VEH. But how could we build a million dollar facility with no construction equipment, no money, and no experienced crew in an impoverished country?

"The army prayed and God moved in miraculous ways. When we needed precision technical-type jobs done or specific raw materials, the right person or equipment came forward, like when a specialized tractor was donated even before we knew we needed it."

The Canadian MFMers' desire to donate a new tractor took John by surprise. "We don't need a tractor," he protested. But God was one jump ahead of him, he now acknowledges, and the tractor arrived in Haiti and filled needs, just as the Lord planned that it should. He knew the building site was eight inches out of grade and while He waited for the builders to discover the problem, He sent along a machine to make it right.

McLaughlin's responsibility load for Operation Saturation turned out to be unmanageably large, at which point God provided as his assistant Dr. Vince Petno, a retired M.D., with a growing, healthy interest in MFMI and therefore, in the world's spiritual needs. Program Director is Petno's title, which meant at the beginning he assumed responsibility for the task force's weekly meetings, a major contribution as the project gathered momentum. He also monitors budgets, handles placement of personnel, and provides liaison with OMS International and other involved agencies.

Early on, MFMI attracted Petno's attention as he worked around OMS International's Indiana headquarters, enjoying nearness to his daughter and son-in-law, Julie and Kurt Bishop, and their children. Kurt serves as the chief financial officer for OMS International.

"I helped them load a truck and saw painted on the side 'Men For Missions.' I remember wondering, What does that mean?"

Vince Petno's curiosity launched his no-turning-back adventure. When he told son-in-law Kurt about his restlessness and discontent with traditional retirement leisure, Kurt began to talk about Operation Saturation and showed Vince the Sonny Solar website.

"I printed out most of the information from the site and spent much time reading about the project and the plight of the Haitians," he says. "God was beginning to draw me in a new way."

In August 2001, "After much prayer, counsel, and the encouragement of my wife," Petno writes, "I explored the possibility of it being the Lord's will that I become a member of the Operation Saturation team." Obviously, the Lord approved (after all, it was His idea in the first place), and Vince says that in the two-plus years on the OpSat team he "had the privilege of seeing God work in marvelous ways. From meetings at OMSI/MFMI headquarters, to prayer and radio distribution in the mountains of Haiti, God's sovereignty and power have been so evident.

"Prior to joining MFMI, I always had a burden for the salvation of family members and friends, but never a world vision. Now after five trips to Haiti and exposure to homeland and foreign missionaries, the Great Commission ("Go into all the world and preach the good news to all creation," Mark 16.15) has taken on a whole new meaning. Although my focus has been Haiti, God has given me and my wife a burden to see all people saved. Over and over again OMSI and MFMI missionaries and friends model this attitude, along with intercessory prayer and practical works."

Petno speaks of learning about spiritual warfare, for he found himself in personal battle as soon as he assumed responsibility within the Operation Saturation project in 2002.

Did the warfare deal him a spiritual setback? Apparently not.

"The last two years," Vince Petno asserts, "have been some of the most challenging and richest of my life. I have been so inspired as I get up close to missionaries who have placed all on the altar...for Christ's sake. I thank God for the way He first led our son-in-law Kurt and daughter Julie to OMS and how that event has so changed my life."

Jim Acheson, from Elkhart, Indiana, knows about change in his life as well. A veteran of a visit to his daughter, Christine, in Colombia, MFMI's business seminar forays into Russia and other former countries of the Soviet Union, expansive horizons were nothing new to him.

Then came Haiti and Operation Saturation.

Some confusion exists as to how the tall, thoughtful Acheson took on responsibility for construction of the new 4VEH studio building. Warren Hardig claims that Jim volunteered for the job, but Jim tells a different story. "I left the meeting to go to the men's room," he claims. "When I came back, I had the job." In any case, Jim Acheson, with years of construction experience, and wife Kay, a successful businesswoman, took on that job with enough gusto to move a mountain.

Which is what needed done, it seems. A logistical mountain, at least. Hardig says that at the building site, "We had no water, no sewer, no power, and no way to communicate."

Acheson elaborates: "There were no final plans, no building materials and no work force in place. And the biggest impediment of all, there was NO MONEY. This defies logic but God and MFMI prevailed."

What then *did* they have?

The Achesons, that's what. Two people who for months put in over 50-hour work weeks so that God's good news could be broadcast across the rock-bound mountains, squalid city streets, seaside coves, and offshore islands of Haiti. Hard work, that, without experienced construction workers nor the equipment North Americans consider basic necessities to put up such a structure.

"All we had to start on," Jim remembers, "was a vision, a preliminary concept, and the faith that God would bless this effort.

"The call went out from MFMI headquarters," Acheson writes. "They came from all over the U.S. and Canada. The marketing team and financial donors stepped to the plate. A number of vendors and suppliers provided materials at cost. Material and supplies were shipped via cargo containers from the U.S. Work crews started coming...and by mid-2001 the project was basically finished."

A 12,500 square foot broadcast facility with state-of-the-art equipment, one of the finest buildings in Cap Haitien, completes the first step in Operation Saturation. An impossibility, most believed, but there it stands, shining in the sun, drawing Haitians to the Savior. Hard work? For sure. Ridiculous odds? Certainly.

But then, almost nothing has gone smoothly for the men and women who are taking on the battle for spiritual freedom in Haiti. Communication amongst them--e-mails, mainly--found in huge white three-ring notebooks in the director's office, reveal ups and downs, discouragement and elation, occasional disagreement or misunderstanding, and remarkable oneness of heart.

The team grappled with strategies. They were forced to hammer through a myriad of funding and promotional ideas. Should they invest in spot ads on Christian radio? What about direct mail requests for funds? Is anyone representing the project in mission-minded churches? Charitable foundations?

Issues and details were endless. A flock of MFMers worked on Sonny Solar materials and even created his own website, along with other promotional efforts. Given their collective business acumen combined with Christian dedication and great vision, the ideas and the authority with which they presented them could be overwhelming. But love and regard seem to reign amongst them. John McLaughlin writes to Warren Hardig, following up their discussion on the issues:

"Well said, Warren. I praise God for all your determination and dedication."

Getting enough people to manage and implement the project was huge. So was/is the business of communicating and coordinating every facet of the effort. Reams of paper, hours of phone calls, days of meetings to keep the army all moving in the same direction. McLaughlin put it in perspective after a visit to Haiti and the site:

"Construction on the new radio station for 4VEH is going well. This is an exciting project. I think all of us at OMS/MFMI have a unique opportunity to be part of God's plan to do something bigger than any of us can imagine."

The new studio building, built with MFMI-generated money and filled with some of the finest equipment available to broadcasting, was dedicated in June 2001. The old studio, bought also by MFM in the late 50s for $10,000, was retired at last from duty.

Emmanuel Felix, a law professor and experienced 4VEH broadcaster, had "agreed in 1999 to be Haitian liaison for OpSat. He organized radio distribution strategies and integrated them into the extension/evangelism aspect for 4VEH ministry," this from Studio Manager Marilyn Shaferly to the 4VEH board.

And Felix, well aware of all that is required to make Operation Saturation happen, wrote in the spring of 2001, "The struggles are hard and costly, but victory is sure!"

OMS International administrators and MFMers spent days in the launching of the project to mesh the mechanics of the generation and management of the thousands of dollars required for the project. Do we set up new accounts, or do we use current ones? Who manages the OpSat accounts? Who is authorized to pay for purchasing and shipping? Who decides what we buy and what we don't buy?

After some of those efforts to divide up responsibility and authority, John McLaughlin wrote to OMS International Vice-President David Dick, "I sense a tremendous spirit of cooperation between all. I can't tell you how pleased I am with your insight and support."

The financial tight spots put a choke chain on everyone involved in the project with disappointing regularity. The word goes out: We're over budget on studio furnishings... Who will pay for those visitors' logistics? Looks like we have to cut $2500 from our monthly allotment. As they faced a

$50,000 shortfall, the primary question before the team was, "How do we bring in more money?"

McLaughlin applied his sense of the big picture yet again, when he wrote, "The task is so overwhelming but so is the potential. It takes a lot of faith to keep the anxiety from setting in that we might let the Lord down."

In March 2001, missionary Marilyn Shaferly sent the team a spiritual shot in the arm about financial difficulties, citing the 14th chapter of Exodus. "May the Lord help us all to get past Exodus 14:11,12 (which is where the Israelites grumble in terror to Moses, and tell him, 'It would have been better for us to serve the Egyptians than to die in the desert')...and on to verses 13 through 15, and God's deliverance and victory (here Moses tells his frightened followers, 'Stand firm and you will see the deliverance the Lord will bring you today...The Lord will fight for you; you need only to be still...'). God has determined that He will be honored."

David Dick added his seasoned analysis: "OpSat is moving along rather well from our far-away perspective. There are hindrances and obstacles but that shouldn't surprise us due to the nature and purpose of the project. Recently I was reminded once again that we battle not against flesh and blood but principalities and powers in high places...."

Within the year the good word came in a Steering Committee meeting that "all projects for OpSat presently have positive fund balances."

When asked after the dedication if the new studio was all paid for, Hardig replied, "Yes."

"How much of its cost was covered by MFMI?"

"All of it."

"And the cost was...?"

"$571,185.80," came his answer. But that's not all. "...plus 20,000 hours of volunteer labor."

Communication among the team members reveals strong desire to create oneness amongst OMSI and MFMI administrators and staffers. Add to the mix gifted, godly Christian leaders in the Haitian community; coupled with them are Haiti missionaries and hundreds of lay people offering their skills and love on behalf of Haiti. These are people who ache over the plight of an island nation whose leader wanted to re-dedicate it to Satan. Getting this diverse collection of high achievers, of "chiefs" (Warren says there is scarcely a follower in the bunch) on the same page and then moving in the same direction was a feat only the world's Creator could accomplish—which He did.

Ed Moore, one of the technical advisers on the project, wrote to his project director about his view of what was happening.

"Thanks for your specific involvement to help keep communication channels open, with resolve and to encourage having an effective team. It is difficult to operate as a scattered group with poor communications, at best. We all continue to need God's hand upon us and His spirit bringing us and the project together.

"I say, praise the Lord for each one involved and for what He is doing through all of us for Haiti!! I am copying my comments to others, because we are a team and will have much to do together in the future...God bless us all."

Warren Hardig says that from the beginning, the team frequently sent up the petition, "Lord, protect our friendships."

The friendships, the relationships thus protected by prayer come under the canopy of grace John McLaughlin described to the Haiti radio board as he reviewed the purposes of OpSat in 2003.

"Wayne King and Gene Bertolet in their marketing and prayer presentation...gave me new inspiration but also caused me to do some soul searching. They emphasized that OpSat is all about prayer. The focus is prayer. It began with prayer. It *was* prayer and today it is [still] a matter of prayer. Our success depends on prayer."

Prayer. Always prayer. Weapon of choice for the stalwarts, men and women, whose maximum effort engages the forces of evil with a stranglehold on the people of Haiti. The days march by, the clock ticks off the minutes. Will they succeed, these warriors giving every ounce of energy, every drop of adrenaline? Will they change the destiny of a nation? Will Satan's grip on Haiti be destroyed? And what will it mean there, if it is?

It's hard to conceive the changes possible when spiritual warfare overcomes evil with good. We're not used to thinking in that magnitude. Our minds can more easily wrap themselves about change, about Satan defeated in one life, one person, one situation.

And that's exactly what is happening in Haiti.

Chapter Fourteen

YonYon

David and RaeLeen Bustin of the Evangelical Bible Mission live and work near the south coast of Haiti. David's grandfather founded Radio 4VEH; the Bustins are cooperating with Men For Missions International and OMS International in Operation Saturation. The first of five downlinks for the station is located in their precinct and operating with their help.

At Christmastime 2003, RaeLeen sent MFMers in Indiana a story that incarnates what is happening as the Lord works with his people to change a nation...one individual at a time.

"Tuesday evening," RaeLeen writes, "our family and church people enjoyed caroling from hut to hut, carrying small kerosene lamps. We even went to the witch doctor's home. It was so beautiful seeing 60 to 70 lamps going down the road.

"On Christmas Eve we went to sleep with the beating voodoo drums all around us. Christmas and Easter are the worst times for voodoo ceremonies.

"Then Christmas arrived! Excitement ran high in our home, as the children had been counting down the days. We enjoyed the morning...so much with little ones. We'd planned a relaxing afternoon until our assistant director, Dinel, came with the news that the local witch doctor had been severely beaten while attending a voodoo dance Christmas Eve.

"I went with Dinel to help. After a long walk down the main road we took a rugged and slippery path to where the man was lying. Before I saw him, I could smell him. My heart sank. I knew it was going to be bad.

"There lay YonYon, the witch doctor, covered in blood, his eye knocked out of his head, his finger hanging, and open wounds all over his arm and head. Bugs fed on the side of his face. I had never seen anything so bad in all my life. They had even passed his body through the fire. Just a few feet away a voodoo ceremony was underway in a little hut. YonYon had laid in the dirt and his blood all night long while his friends continued to dance.

"I walked over to the voodoo service. I saw the witch doctor who was in charge and the man who had beaten YonYon, but you cannot reason with a demon-possessed man. I returned to YonYon where some of the people had already started the death wail. They knew he was dying.

"In hopes that YonYon could hear me, I talked to him about the importance of accepting Jesus as his Savior. Then I told Dinel we had to do something. We could not let him die there in that filth. A man from our church who had gone with us, immediately volunteered to take YonYon in his truck to the hospital. But first we had to carry him, unconscious, back up to the path.

"David has witnessed to YonYon for many years, so he knows about the Savior. At dinner that Christmas evening with church leaders and their families, a neighbor told me that YonYon had promised to accept Jesus as his Savior after he gets the radio, speaking of the Radio 4VEH fix-tuned, solar radios being given to Haitian people.

"As I walked back home, my heart was heavy for this country. I prayed that God would truly deliver these people from the clutches of Satan."

After he gets his radio. He promised to accept Jesus as his Savior after he gets the radio. All the way from Wayne King's vision for Haiti, through the prayer, the planning, the countless hours of work, the goal was this: that YonYon find relief and release from evil, YonYon and every other Haitian who pins tattered hopes to their worst enemy, Satan. A small steady light in his darkness gave YonYon hope that help lay within the words and music from a small radio he could hold in his hand.

Three days after Christmas, RaeLeen Bustin sent another bulletin, bursting with triumph and joy, about Yon-Yon's situation.

"I have great news! YonYon accepted Jesus as his Savior in the clinic. David has prayed for this guy for years. He was SO excited! Please ask everyone to pray hard for YonYon. He has a long way to go.

"David was with him all day Friday. When I got YonYon to the path on Christmas Day I had him sent to the local facility even though I knew they couldn't help him. It was better for him than lying in the dirt.

"On Friday David took him to Cayes to an American doctor's clinic. The doctor confirmed that YonYon's eye is gone, but he was able to talk. David said while he was there he prayed very seriously even after being unconscious for more than 30 hours."

David picks up the story. "While the missionary doctor was examining YonYon, I was witnessing to him about

God's great love for him and his need to accept Jesus as his Savior. While lying on the exam table, YonYon accepted Jesus into his heart! You could feel the presence of God's angels all around us.

"Five weeks later YonYon came to our home to visit...WOW! What a changed man! He could not say enough words of praise for all God did for him. He said, 'I know God is my Savior. He knows all He is doing and He does all things well.'

"He expressed how Satan, his headmaster, had taken many times more from him than he had given him. God is blessing his soul so much he can hardly contain the joy in his heart. He said, 'My sins are forgiven and God keeps cleansing me.'

"YonYon told about all the voodoo items he used in his practice. He said he has them all gathered up; some he cannot touch as they have demon spirits in them. He asked me to come to his home...to burn all of his voodoo items. God is working miracles in Haiti!!!"

RaeLeen ends her tale of YonYon's final freedom with a request: "Pray without ceasing....Believe to see Haiti turn to Jesus. YonYon's conversion should strengthen our faith in the One who is faithful."

This is not the end of the story, either for YonYon or Operation Saturation. Faith in the hearts of thousands of gutsy, hard-working guys is making it possible for YonYon, and others like him, to take shelter in the Savior.

When Warren Hardig wrote his report for the Men For Missions International Cabinet at the end of 2003, it came straight from his overloaded heart. He speaks of his personal goal for MFMI to send "78 prayer teams annually to OMSI fields. I hope we can bring the ministry team numbers to 1,000 members a year." (In 2003 there were 76 U.S. teams with 445 people to 13 countries, according to Hardig's report. This doesn't count those from Canada, South Africa and the United Kingdom.)

Warren also updated the cabinet on the status of OpSat.

"Operation Saturation is making a difference in the country of Haiti. Pastor Codo...said, 'Every day people are coming to Christ through the radios.' Only eternity will reveal the effectiveness of Radio 4VEH. The listening audience...has increased to over 600,000 people.

"From the radio distribution, 3,482 people have prayed to receive Christ. On my last prayer team trip in October, we were privileged to pray with a witch doctor, his wife, his niece, and his assistant along with five other people in the brief time we were there. In follow-up, we know of at least 40 people who have prayed to receive Christ as the result of just one radio. One of those 40 was a witch doctor and...he has taken down the signs of voodoo, and severed relationship with one of his two wives. He is taking care of her financially, however, and provides a home for her without further involvement."

The timbers that bear the weight of everything done lie in the report's opening paragraph, a clear, strong goal statement from the director's heart:

"I want Men For Missions International to always be about the lordship of Jesus Christ in each person's life, at home and around the world."

The MFMI story isn't over—not by a long shot. Even when Operation Saturation is history, as long as men show up who are willing to do, go, and give on behalf of those without Jesus, somewhere in the world God has a job tailored for each one.

After all, that's what Men For Missions International is all about.

Retrospect

The Men For Missions International's 50-year-long story interests me in part because it occurred during my lifetime; I lived much of it as an OMS missionary in Korea and before that as founder Dwight Ferguson's daughter. As I began work on this book, however, the researcher/writer in me took over and I began to look at MFMI from a broader perspective.

At how Dwight Ferguson's reluctance evolved into relentless passion.

At how some of the original laymen view that day in July 1954, and what God put into motion then.

I also discovered some of the weight-bearing pillars that enable MFMI to stand strong and then to soar, according to God's purposes. Significant characteristics wind like valley streams through the growth, the change, and the vitality that is Men For Missions International.

One is prayer. The first thing that original band of men did as they gathered to hear what Ferguson had to say was pray. To this day prayer surrounds and saturates every trip, every project, every decision. Cabinet meetings begin and end with prayer. In their meetings, neighborhood councils include prayer for missionaries and for each other as part of their purpose. Banquets. Committees. Moments of sharing faith. All imprinted with prayer.

And spiritual growth seems always to percolate at the heart of MFMI action. Retreats, yes, where Bible studies and prayer sessions bring a man face to face with God's measuring rod. But beside these, association with other godly guys seems to give the Holy Spirit multiplied chances to nudge men into a deeper walk with the Lord. Hearing someone acknowledge publicly his broken heart over spiritually needy folk has opened more than a few hearts toward greater faith, stronger commitment.

Even men without personal faith have found themselves for whatever reason pitched headlong into a ministry team headed for faraway places. And before the work was finished, the hot blue flames of their teammates' desire to tell the world about Jesus warmed and transformed them as well.

Deep and abiding fellowship is a characteristic of MFMI. Warren Hardig's prayer, which underlies all the work of Operation Saturation, attests to that. "Lord, protect our friendships." He knows something of inestimable worth would die if relationships were to rupture over funds or decision-making or power.

And more, the flame that burns within the heart and soul of Men For Missions International often ignites the men and women who stand too close. It blazes up in them as it has done in others countless times before, stirring them to action, to utilizing their skills and talents for "the only cause that matters."

When Dr. David Dick, OMSI Vice President for International Ministries, was questioned about MFMI's contribution to OMS International ministries, he replied,

"It's critical. Our career people are overworked, so non-resident missionaries (that's how he views MFMers) contribute so much. They are very important. In Japan, for instance, MFMers upgraded and renovated facilities. They represent prayer support. It's a case, I think, of prayer, personnel, projects."

And speaking from the middle of the Operation Saturation project, with all its details and dreams, Dick looks on it as "an entrepreneurial leap of faith, one I pray we can see working in other countries. As we've done it in Haiti and, given the resources developed there—Sonny Solar, prayer, manpower, for instance—I can see it happening elsewhere, another try at reaching a whole nation with the Christian gospel."

It sounds as if the first 50 years of Men For Missions International forged a launching pad for future forays into doing God's work in His waiting world.

As Harry Burr, retired and frequently retreaded MFMI patriarch, says, "We've only just begun."

Glossary of Terms

ACTION Magazine: A quarterly publication of Men For Missions International. A free subscription can be obtained by writing MFMI, P. O. Box A, Greenwood, IN 46142.

Associate Staff: Laymen who are neither lay missionaries nor employees of OMS. They volunteer their services and are not included in regular missionary benefits. They are appointed by the MFMI cabinet for two-year terms.

Cabinet: Made up of men representing all parts of the United States, the Cabinet establishes policy and gives direction to MFMI. There is also an international cabinet.

Council:

A regional group of laymen and pastors who meet monthly to assist the work of MFMI through prayer, raising funds to provide financial support, conducting retreats and banquets, and sending council members on crusades.

Crusade or
Team Director:

A member of the MFMI staff who leads overseas trips for ministry.

Men For Missions
International:

The Laymen's Voice of OMS International. Through MFMI thousands of men from multiple church affiliations and every walk of life have found a channel for harnessing and releasing personal skills and abilities in practical, direct missionary involvement. No dues are required, and membership is open to any man who pledges: I will do whatever God asks me to do; I will go wherever God asks me to go; I will give whatever God asks me to give.

MFMI:

Men For Missions International, P.O. Box A, Greenwood, IN 46142, 317/881-6752. The initials are often shortened to MFM.

OMS International:

OMS International (OMSI) is a faith mission which stands in the historic evangelical tradition of the church. In response to the Great Commission, OMS emphasizes evangelism, training of and partnership with national leadership for ministry, and church planting. Copies of OMS Articles of Faith are available by writing OMS International, P.O. Box A, Greenwood, IN 46142.

Operation Saturation (OpSat):

Operation Saturation is a five-year, seven-phase plan to reach Haiti for Christ through small, fix-tuned, solar-powered radios:

1. Construct and equip a new broadcast center.

2. Build digital satellite uplink and downlink sites to reach all of Haiti.

3. Saturate Haiti with thousands of small fix-tuned, solar-powered radios.

4. Launch an evangelistic radio campaign to reach Haiti through the fix-tuned radios.

5. Minister to new believers, new and existing churches, while training Haitian laypeople to reach their own country.

Regional Directors:	MFMI regional directors assist the national director by implementing and supervising the activities of MFMI within their geographic areas.
79ers:	Refers to Penetration '79 known as *Impacto* in Ecuador, where 37 MFMers from the U.S. gave a month in 1979 to evangelism in three major cities—resulting in over 1000 decisions for Christ and establishing three new churches.
Sonny Solar:	Sonny Solar is the mascot for Operation Saturation. He is a cartoon replica of the solar powered radios that are being sent to Haiti to spread the Gospel of Jesus Christ. Sonny "The 'Son' Powered Missionary" is the creation of Wayne King and Gene Bertolet. Sonny's job is to

get himself sent to Haiti with as many of his relatives as possible through his mission, "Operation Saturation." Through living out his mission, he hopes to introduce children to missions and the power of prayer.

Other Books by Men For Missions International

Iron Sharpens Iron	by Warren G. Hardig
Impacto!	by Lee Huffman
Motivated Men	by Dwight Ferguson
Men Plus God	by B. H. Pearson